KM

COME AGAIN

COOKIE BOOK

by Evelyn Birkby

Easy-to-make, carefree, healthy, prizewinners and other special recipes for cookies taken from those brought to KMA's Fall Festivals since the publication of the popular KMA **Festival Cookie Book**.

Published by
KMA Broadcasting, L.P.
Box 960
Shenandoah, Iowa 51601

© **1987**
All Rights Reserved
ISBN 0-9615083-2-9

Printed by:
BRENNAN PRINTING
100 Main Street
Deep River, Iowa 52222

FOREWORD

Welcome to KMA'S **COME AGAIN COOKIE BOOK**. Like the other cookbooks from KMA, we promise you enjoyable reading, interesting food ideas, ease of preparation and, of course, the fun of eating.

My wife Carrie and our son Ben looked forward to this book as much as I. Carrie likes to bake and Ben and I like to eat. Besides, some of the recipes are simple enough that I might try my hand at making them myself. When Ben is old enough, he just might make a good cookie-making helper in the kitchen for us both.

When I am given a choice, I usually say my favorites are the chocolate chip, oatmeal and raisins, and the peanut butter cookies. No doubt most of you would consider these "traditional" recipes. Those kinds are in this book to be sure, but also many are upbeat and "modern" combinations. In fact, it seems to me that this book has in it something for everyone, no matter what your taste or lifestyle.

All of us at KMA send our best wishes and hope you enjoy the **COME AGAIN COOKIE BOOK** for many, many years.

Happy cookie making,

Ed May, Jr.

Ed May Jr.
General Partner, KMA Broadcasting, L.P.

INTRODUCTION

Here we come again!

You asked for this book taken from the thousands of cookie recipes which our radio friends brought to the famous KMA Fall Festivals since the publication of the **Festival Cookie Book**. Recipes for a wide variety of types, styles and ingredients are included. Some are variations of old favorites; some are brand new ideas using the latest techniques and equipment. The entire book contains treasured cookie recipes for your use.

Included are all the winners from the contest which was held at the most recent Fall Festival plus special prizewinners from the Iowa State Fair.

I want to express my appreciation fo Radio Station KMA for recognizing the value of such publications and the willingness to build on the success of the **Festival Cookie Book** and **Cooking with KMA; Featuring 60 Years of Radio Homemakers** to venture out with a third cookbook, the **Come Again Cookie Book**. My appreciation to Darrell Murphy, Director of Special Events/Station Promotions, who assisted and encouraged as the book grew from words on those thousands of recipe cards to the printed pages. A special thanks to Arlette Hollister, Food Superintendent for the Iowa State Fair, for permission to print the prizewinning fair recipes included. And a heartfelt thanks to all the people who have attended the KMA Festivals through the years and brought their cookies and recipes--this is truly your book.

We trust that you will use these recipes with pleasure and **COME AGAIN** to KMA as often as you can with the knowledge that we are close friends.

With Best Regards,

Evelyn Birkby

SECTION INDEX

..A LOOK AHEAD–

Judges Ester Mae Cox, Iowa State Home Economist from Bedford, Iowa, (on the right) and Thelma Heitsman, Consultant with Okey/Vernon Company of Corning, Iowa, display some of the Cookie Contest winners at the KMA Fall Festival. Evelyn Birkby of KMA, (Chairman of the Cookie Contest) is at the left announcing the names of the winners.

PRIZE WINNERS

PRIZEWINNERS

At the most recent KMA Fall Festival, a cookie contest was held with delightful and delicious results. The following are the prize winners. The contestants decided into which categories the recipes should be placed.

━━━━━━━━━━━━━━━

FIRST PLACE APRICOT BAR

¾ cup margarine
1 cup sugar
2 cups flour
½ tsp. salt
½ tsp. soda
2 cups dried apricots
Water to cover apricots
¾ cup sugar
1⅓ cups flaked coconut
½ cup chopped English walnuts
¼ tsp. almond flavoring

Cream together the margarine and 1 cup sugar. Sift flour, salt and soda together and mix into creamed mixture. Spread 3 cups of mixture into a greased 10x15-inch pan. Pat smooth. Bake at 400 degrees for about 10 minutes. Place apricots in pan, cover with water and simmer until most of the water is absorbed. Stir in ¾ cup sugar and continue cooking until thick. Cool. Stir in coconut, nuts and flavoring. Spread over baked layer. Sprinkle remaining crumb mixture over top. Can add more nuts and coconut if desired. Bake at 400 degrees about 15 minutes or until light brown. Cool. Cut into squares or bars. Yield: 4 dozen. (1st place, Bar Cookies--Norma Schaaf, Randolph, IA)

━━━━━━━━━━━━━━━

PEANUT BUTTER TREATS

½ cup butter, softened
½ cup brown sugar, packed
½ cup white sugar
1 egg
½ cup creamy peanut butter
½ tsp. vanilla flavoring
1¼ cups flour
¾ tsp. soda
½ tsp. salt
36 miniature peanut butter chocolate
  cups

Combine butter, sugars, egg, peanut butter and flavoring in mixing bowl; beat until smooth. Combine flour, soda and salt; add to creamed mixture. Roll into 36 small balls the size of a walnut; put each in a small, greased muffin tin. Make a depression in each. Bake at 375 degrees for 8 to 9 minutes. Remove from oven. Immediately put a peanut butter cup in each cookie. Cool for 10 minutes. Twist gently to remove from pan. Cool on rack. Store in cool place. Yield: 36. (2nd Place, Filled Cookies--Violet Bredensteiner, Northboro, IA)

JEAN'S WINNING BARS

1 cup flour
½ cup butter or margarine
¼ cup sugar
1 cup graham cracker crumbs
½ cup chocolate chips
½ cup chopped nuts
1 tsp. baking powder
¼ tsp. salt
14-oz. can sweetened condensed milk

Heat oven to 350 degrees. Lightly spoon flour into measuring cup, level off. In a small bowl, cut margarine into flour and sugar until crumbly. Press into 9x13-inch ungreased pan. Bake at 350 degrees for 10 minutes. Cool 10 minutes. In a large bowl combine cracker crumbs, chocolate chips, chopped nuts, baking powder, salt and sweetened condensed milk. Mix well. Spread over partially baked crust. Return to oven and bake 15 to 20 minutes or until golden brown. Cool. Top with the following frosting:

Frosting

1½ cups powdered sugar
½ cup butter or margarine
1 tsp. vanilla flavoring

Blend until creamy; spread over bars. Yield: 36 bars. (3rd place, Bar Cookies--Mrs. Stanley Olson, Red Oak, IA)

FROSTED CARROT BARS

2 eggs
1 cup sugar
1 cup sifted flour
1 tsp. soda
1 tsp. cinnamon
½ tsp. salt
¾ cup cooking oil
1½ cups finely grated carrots
¾ cup coconut
¾ cup chopped pecans

Beat eggs until light, gradually beat in sugar. Sift dry ingredients together and add alternately with oil. Mix well. Fold in remaining ingredients. Spread in greased 9x13-inch pan. Bake at 350 degrees for 25 to 30 minutes. Frost with the following:

Butter Frosting

¼ cup butter or margarine
2 Tbls. milk
1 tsp. vanilla flavoring
2 cups powdered sugar

Combine butter or margarine and milk in pan and heat until blended and hot. Remove from heat; add flavoring and stir into powdered sugar. Spread over bars and sprinkle with more pecans if desired. (2nd place, Bar Cookies--Mary Hoffman, Arcadia, IA)

COCONUT JOYS

½ cup margarine
2 cups powdered sugar
3 cups coconut (18 oz.)
2 1-oz. sq. unsweetened chocolate

Melt margarine, add sugar and coconut. Shape into circles. Make indentation in center. Fill centers with melted chocolate (or melted cherry chips or semi-sweet chocolate chips--or use your imagination). DO NOT BAKE. Chill and store in refrigerator. Yield: 3 dozen (2nd Place, Refrigerator--Ruth Rannebeck, Falls City, NE)

CREAM WAFERS

1 cup softened butter
⅓ cup cream (35% butter fat)
2 cups sifted flour

Combine ingredients and mix well. Chill. Roll out dough to 1/8-inch thick on floured board. Cut with 1½-inch cutter. (Roll only ⅓ of dough at a time. Keep remainder refrigerated.) Place rounds on wax paper heavily coated with white sugar; turn each round so both sides are coated with sugar. Place on ungreased baking sheet. Prick with fork about 4 times. Bake at 375 degrees for 7 to 9 minutes until just done. Cool. Put two cookies together with the following:

Frosting

¼ cup softened butter
¾ cup sifted powdered sugar
1 egg yolk
1 tsp. vanilla flavoring
Food coloring as desired

Combine ingredients and blend well. Tint as desired (pink and green are pretty). Make into little sandwiches. (4th Place, Filled Cookies--Dorothy Bay, Shenandoah, IA)

PECAN TASSIES

3-oz. pkg. cream cheese
½ cup butter or margarine
1 cup sifted flour
Dash of salt
⅔ cups chopped pecans
1 tsp. vanilla flavoring
2 eggs
¾ cup brown sugar
1 Tbls. soft butter

Soften cream cheese to room temperature. Blend in ½ cup butter and stir in flour and salt. Chill for 1 hour. Shape into 24 one-inch balls. Place in small muffin tins and press down into shape of tin. Put several pecan pieces in bottom of each. Beat remaining ingredients together and pour over pecan pieces. Bake at 325 degrees for 25 minutes. (1st Place, Filled Cookies--Wilma Windhorst, Tarkio, MO)

INEXPENSIVE MOLASSES COOKIES

½ cup shortening
1 cup sugar
1 cup molasses
½ cup water
4 cups flour
1½ tsp. ginger
1 tsp. soda
1 tsp. salt
1 tsp. cloves
1 tsp. nutmeg
½ tsp. allspice

Cream shortening and sugar. Beat in molasses and water. Sift dry ingredients together and add. Chill dough. Roll out ¼-inch thick on floured board. Cut into 3-inch circles. Place on greased baking sheet. Sprinkle with sugar. Press a raisin in center of each. Bake at 350 degrees for 10 to 12 minutes. Can make "spokes" of icing radiating out from center of each baked cookie. Yield: 2½ dozen. (2nd Place, Rolled and Cut--Mrs. Bob Werner, Salem, NE)

CHOCOLATE SPRILL COOKIES

1 cup powdered sugar
1 cup butter
1 tsp. vanilla flavoring
1½ cups sifted flour
½ tsp. baking powder
1/8 tsp. salt
1 cup rolled oats
Chocolate sprills

Cream sugar, butter and flavoring together. Add dry ingredients in order given. Shape into rolls or logs. Roll to coat in chocolate sprills. Chill until dough can be cut into slices. Bake on greased cookie sheets at 325 degrees for 15 to 20 minutes. (4th Place, Refrigerator--Mary Tallmon, Creston, IA)

GINGER COOKIES

1½ cups sifted flour
1 tsp. soda
1½ tsp. ginger
1 tsp. cinnamon
¼ tsp. cloves
Dash of salt
¼ cup butter
¼ cup margarine
¾ cup sugar
1 egg
1½ tsp. dark corn syrup
Whole almonds

Sift flour, soda and spices together and set aside. Cream butter and margarine with sugar; beat in egg and corn syrup. When fluffy, blend in dry ingredients. Roll on lightly floured board. Cut in shapes desired and put one almond on top of each cookie. Bake on greased baking sheet on top shelf of oven at 375 degrees for 6 to 8 minutes. Watch closely, do not over-bake. (1st Place, Rolled and Cut--Evelyn Verpoorten, Avoca, IA)

PEARL'S CHEESE BARS

1 regular-size box yellow cake mix
1 stick butter or margarine, melted
3 eggs
1 cup chopped pecans
8-oz. pkg. cream cheese
16-oz. box powdered sugar
1 tsp. vanilla flavoring

Combine cake mix, melted butter or margarine, 1 egg and pecans. Beat at low speed until well blended. Spoon mixture into 8x11- or 9-inch square baking pan and press evenly. Set aside. Combine remaining two eggs, cream cheese, sugar and flavoring. Beat at medium speed until soft and creamy. Pour on top of first layer. Bake at 325 degrees for 40 to 50 minutes, or until center is set and top is lightly browned. Remove from oven and cool on wire rack. Cut into squares or bars. Yield: 30 bars. (4th Place, Bar Cookies--Mrs. Orlin Hutt, Shenandoah, IA)

CHERRY WINKS

1 regular-size cherry cake mix
¼ cup margarine
¼ tsp. butter flavoring
8-oz. pkg. cream cheese
1 egg white, stiffly beaten
¼ cup chopped nuts
¼ cup coconut

Mix half of cake mix with margarine and butter flavoring in mixer. When smooth, fold in beaten egg white and remaining half of cake mix. Stir in nuts and coconut. Drop by teaspoon onto ungreased cookie sheet. Bake at 375 degrees for 8 to 10 minutes. (1st Place, Miscellaneous--Leona Dorn, Adams NE)

PEANUT BUTTER SWIRLS

½ cup shortening
1 cup sugar
½ cup chunky peanut butter
1 egg
2 Tbls. milk
1½ cup flour
½ tsp. salt
½ tsp. soda
6-oz. pkg. chocolate chips

Cream shortening and sugar until light. Beat in peanut butter, egg and milk. Sift dry ingredients together and stir into creamed mixture. Place dough on lightly floured waxed paper. Roll out to 15x8-inch rectangle. Melt chocolate chips over hot water or in microwave; spread over dough. Roll up like jelly roll, lifting wax paper slightly with each turn. Let chill 20 minutes. Slice ¼-inch thick and bake on greased cookie sheet at 375 degrees for 8 to 10 minutes. (3rd Place, Filled Cookies--Helen Schilling, Northboro, IA)

CHOCOLATE CHIP PEANUT BUTTER COOKIE

½ cup brown sugar, packed
½ cup butter or margarine, softened
½ cup honey
½ cup chunky peanut butter
1 egg
1 tsp. vanilla flavoring
2½ cups flour
½ tsp. soda
½ tsp. salt
6-oz. pkg. chocolate chips

Cream brown sugar and margarine in mixer at medium speed. Blend in honey, peanut butter, egg and flavoring. Lightly spoon flour into measuring cup, level top with knife. Blend flour, soda and salt into creamed mixture. Stir in chips. Refrigerate. Shape into 1-inch balls. Place on greased cookie sheets. Flatten with fork dipped in sugar. Bake at 350 degrees for 8 to 12 minutes or until golden brown. Yield: 5½ dozen. (3rd Place, Refrigerator--Ruth Hauser, Conception Junction, MO)

CANDY BAR COOKIES

¾ cup butter or margarine
¾ cup sifted powdered sugar
1 tsp. vanilla flavoring
2 Tbls. evaporated milk
¼ tsp. salt
2 cups flour

Cream butter and gradually add sugar. Mix well. Add flavoring, milk and salt. Stir in flour. Roll out on lightly floured board, using half of dough at a time, to 1/8 inch thick. Cut into rectangles. Put on ungreased cookie sheet. Bake at 325 degrees for 12 to 15 minutes.

Caramel Filling

½ lb. caramel candy
¼ cup evaporated milk
¼ cup butter or margarine
1 cup sifted powdered sugar
1 cup chopped pecans (optional)

Combine caramels and milk in top of double boiler. When melted, add remaining ingredients. Keep unused portion over hot water; spread caramel layer on each cookie.

Chocolate Icing

1 cup chocolate chips
¼ cup evaporated milk
2 Tbls. butter
½ tsp. vanilla flavoring
½ cup powdered sugar

Melt chocolate and milk in double boiler. Remove from heat but keep over hot water; add remaining ingredients. Frost over top of caramel layer. (3rd Place, Rolled and Cut--Mrs. Joe O'Hara, Shenandoah, IA.)

ITALIAN ANISE COOKIE (BISCOTTI)

5 cups flour
5 tsp. baking powder
1 cup sugar
½ tsp. salt
¾ cup oil
¾ cup liquid (juice of 1 orange plus milk)
Grated rind of 1 orange
2 eggs
1 tsp. anise flavoring

Sift dry ingredients together. Beat liquid ingredients together and stir into dry ingredients. Pinch off dough the size of walnuts and form into rope twists, circles or any shape desired. Place on ungreased cookie sheet and bake at 450 degrees for 7 to 8 minutes. (3rd Place, Miscellaneous--Pauline Gilard, Shenandoah, IA)

FAVORITE SUGAR COOKIES

1½ cups sugar
1 cup shortening
2 large eggs
1 tsp. vanilla flavoring
1 tsp. soda
½ tsp. salt
About 4 cups flour

Combine ingredients in the order given. Mix well. Add only enough flour to handle well. Roll out on lightly floured board and cut with cookie cut-ter. Place on greased cookie sheet and bake 10 to 12 minutes at 350 degrees. (4th Place, Rolled and Cut--Darlene Kimmen, Harlan, IA)

SANTA'S WHISKERS

1 cup butter or margarine, softened
1 cup sugar
2 Tbls. milk
1 tsp. vanilla or rum flavoring
2½ cups sifted flour
¾ cups finely chopped red candied or maraschino cherries
½ cup finely chopped pecans
Flaked coconut for coating

Cream together the butter or margarine and sugar. Blend in milk and flavoring; add alternately with flour. Stir in cherries and nuts. (If maraschino cherries are used, drain and pat dry.) Form dough into 2 or 3 rolls. Roll in coconut to coat. Wrap in wax paper and chill thoroughly. Slice ¼-inch thick and bake on ungreased cookie sheet in a preheated 375 degree oven until edges are golden brown--about 10 minutes. Yield: 50. (1st Place, Refrigerator--Delores Harrington, Tarkio, MO)

-13-

COCONUT NESTS

2 cups powdered sugar
½ cup butter or margarine, melted
3 cups flaked coconut
½ cup chocolate chips, melted

Combine sugar, margarine and coconut. Mix well. Form into walnut-sized balls. Flatten slightly and make an indentation in the center of each. Fill center with melted chocolate chips. (1st Place, Unbaked--Mrs. Glenn Peterson, Kiron, IA)

CARE BEARS

1 cup sugar
½ cup butter or margarine
2 eggs
2 cups flour
½ tsp. salt
½ tsp. soda
2 1-oz. sq. unsweetened chocolate, melted
2 tsp. vanilla flavoring

Beat sugar and butter or margarine with electric mixer on high speed until light and fluffy. Beat in eggs. Reduce to low; add dry ingredients. Beat in melted chocolate and flavoring. Shape dough into ball; wrap in plastic wrap and chill until dough is easy to handle. (Or freeze for 40 minutes.)

Divide dough into 12 pieces. Shape each portion as follows: Cut one dough piece in half. Shape half into large ball for bear's body. Place on ungreased cookie sheet; flatten slightly into 3-inch by 2½-inch oval. Cut remaining half in half; shape one piece into small ball and arrange next to large ball, overlapping, for bear's head. From remaining dough, pinch off small piece for nose; place on head. Roll rest of piece of dough into a 5-inch long rope. Cut two ½-inch pieces for ears and cut four 1-inch pieces for legs. Roll each into a ball and press ears and legs in appropriate places next to bear.

Repeat with remaining dough to make 12 bears in all. Bake 8 minutes at 350 degrees. Cool on cookie sheet or wire rack. When cool, frost using decorating bag.

Frosting

1¼ cup powdered sugar
1/8 tsp. cream of tartar
1 egg white

Combine and beat until blended. Continue beating until mixture is so stiff a knife cut into the frosting will leave a clean path. (3rd Place, Shaped and Pressed--Mrs. R. Salomons, Sterling, NE)

EXTRA CRUNCH NO-BAKE COOKIES

1 cup sugar
1 cup white corn syrup
1 cup coconut
2 cups corn flakes (don't crush)
1 cup crunchy peanut butter
7-oz. pkg. chow mein noodles

Cook sugar and syrup together until sugar is dissolved, stirring constantly. Combine remaining ingredients in large greased bowl. Pour in syrup mixture and mix well. Drop by teaspoon on wax paper. When cool, store in tightly covered container in refrigerator. (4th Place, Unbaked--Leona Riebge, Avoca, NE)

QUICK COOKIES

36 caramels
3 Tbls. half-and-half
1 cup coconut
1 cup nuts
1 cup corn flakes
1 cup crispy rice cereal

Melt caramels and half-and-half in top of double boiler. (Water should be hot but not boiling.) Mix remaining ingredients in a greased bowl. Pour caramel mixture over cereal mixture and mix well. Drop by spoonful onto wax paper, let set. (2nd Place Unbaked--Dorothy Martens, Minden, IA)

ALMOND BARK COOKIES

2 lbs. almond bark
1 cup peanut butter
2 cups salted peanuts
3 cups crisp rice cereal
2 cups miniature marshmallows

Melt almond bark in top of double boiler. Stir in peanut butter. When well blended, combine with remaining ingredients. Mix well. Drop by teaspoons on wax paper and set until firm. (3rd Place, Unbaked-Rosa Volkmer, Nebraska City, NE)

KOOKIE BRITTLE

1 cup margarine
1½ tsp. vanilla flavoring
1 tsp. salt
1 cup sugar
2 cups flour
1 cup chocolate chips

Combine margarine, flavoring and salt; blend well. Gradually beat in remaining ingredients. When well mixed, press evenly into ungreased jelly roll pan and bake at 350 degrees for 20 to 23 minutes. Cool. Turn out on paper towels to absorb any excess shortening. Break into irregular pieces. A good choice for mailing. (4th Place--Miscellaneous, Mrs. C.A. Anderson, Albia, IA)

GINGER CREAMS

¼ cup shortening
½ cup sugar
1 egg, beaten
½ cup sorghum
½ cup hot water
1 tsp. soda
2 cups flour
½ tsp. salt
1 tsp. ginger
½ tsp. nutmeg
½ tsp. cloves
½ tsp. cinnamon

Cream shortening and sugar until fluffy. Beat in egg and sorghum. Combine hot water and soda. Stir remaining dry ingredients together and add alternately with soda mixture. Dough will be rather soft. Chill dough. Drop by teaspoon 2-inches apart on lightly greased baking sheet. Bake at 375 degrees for about 8 minutes. Ice while warm with the following icing or with a cream cheese frosting:

Icing

½ cup powdered sugar
A few drops of vanilla flavoring
2 to 3 Tbls. hot milk or coffee

Combine ingredients and mix until thick and smooth. (2nd Place Drop Cookies--Elaine Spargur, Shenandoah, IA)

CHOCOLATE MOUNDS

1¾ cups flour
1 tsp. salt
½ tsp. soda
½ cup cocoa
1 cup sugar
½ cup shortening
1 egg
1 tsp. vanilla flavoring
½ cup milk
½ cup chopped nuts
Marshmallows, cut

Sift flour, salt, soda and cocoa together. Cream sugar and shortening: beat in egg. Add dry ingredients alternately with flavoring and milk. Add nuts. Drop on greased and floured pan; bake at 375 degrees for 4 to 5 minutes. Top each cookie with a marshmallow half; press in gently. Bake 2 minutes. Cool, then glaze with the following:

Glaze

½ cup cocoa
1½ cups sifted powdered sugar
3 Tbls. hot water
⅓ cup melted butter

Combine ingredients and spread over top of marshmallow on baked cookie. (3rd Place, Drop--Mrs. Lewis Sargent, Pacific Junction, IA)

HAPPY HOUSE PECAN KISSES

1 egg white
1 cup brown sugar, packed
1 Tbls. flour
½ tsp. salt
1 cup coarsely chopped pecans

Beat egg until stiff; gradually add combined sugar, flour and salt. Beat constantly until stiff peaks form. Add nuts. Drop by teaspoon onto buttered cookie sheet 2-inches apart. Bake in slow oven, 325 degrees, for 20 minutes or until lightly browned. Do not overbake. Yield: 2 dozen. (4th Place, Drop--Bonnie Routh, Creston, IA)

CHOCOLATE-COVERED FILBERT FINGERS

¾ cup softened butter
¼ cup sugar
½ tsp. vanilla flavoring
1 egg
1 cup flour
½ cup finely chopped filberts
3 1-oz. sq. semi-sweet chocolate
    or a large Hershey bar

Beat butter and sugar together until light and fluffy. Reduce speed to low and add flavoring, egg, then flour and half of the filberts. Preheat oven to 400 degrees. Spoon dough into decorating bag with medium rosette tube. Pipe dough into 2½-inch lengths about 1 inch apart on ungreased cookie sheet. Bake 6 to 8 minutes at 400 degrees or until golden. Remove from cookie sheet and cool. Melt chocolate over low heat. Dip each cookie halfway into chocolate and then into rest of nuts. Place on wax paper and let dry. Keeps in airtight container up to three days. Yield: 2 dozen. (1st Place, Shaped and Pressed--Mildred Finlay, Shenandoah, IA)

KC'S SUGAR COOKIES

1 cup sugar
1 cup butter
2 eggs
1 tsp. vanilla flavoring
½ tsp. butter flavoring
2½ cups flour
½ tsp. salt
1 tsp. baking powder

Cream sugar and butter together; beat in eggs and flavorings. Blend in remaining ingredients. Cover and chill. Roll dough 1/8-inch thick on lightly floured board. Cut into desired shapes with cookie cutters. Place on ungreased baking sheets. Bake at 400 degrees for 6 to 8 minutes or until light brown. Frost if desired. (2nd Place, Shaped and Pressed--Mrs. Kathryn Guest, King City, MO)

The Annual KMA Fall Festival attracts thousands of visitors from the Midwest who share the day, their time, their cookies and their recipes.

CHOCOLATE CHIP COOKIE

1 cup margarine
1 cup white sugar
1 cup brown sugar
2 tsp. vanilla flavoring
2 eggs
3 cups flour
1 tsp. soda
1½ tsp. salt
12-oz. pkg. chocolate chips
Nuts, if desired

Cream margarine and sugars. Add flavoring and eggs and mix thoroughly. Mix dry ingredients together and blend into first mixture. Add chips and nuts. Drop on greased cookie sheet and bake at 375° for 8 to 10 minutes. This cookie should be made with the freshest of ingredients, shaped evenly and baked just enough-

-do not overbake. (Sweepstakes-- Meredith Walker--Elementary Grade School Student--Essex, IA)

SPARKLING GINGERSNAPS

1 cup white sugar
¼ cup butter or margarine
½ cup shortening
1 egg
¼ cup light molasses
2 cups sifted flour
1½ tsp. soda
1 tsp. cinnamon
½ tsp. salt
½ tsp. ginger
½ tsp. allspice
Sugar for coating

Beat sugar, butter or margarine, shortening, egg and molasses together. Add sifted dry ingredients all at once, mixing well. Using a teaspoon, measure each spoonful into a ball. Drop into plate of sugar. Place sugared balls 2½ inches apart on ungreased baking sheet. Bake at 350° for about 12 to 15 minutes or until tops crack. Cool briefly, lift onto wire rack. Puffed cookies flatten as they cool. Store in can with loose-fitting cover. (4th Place--Shaped and Pressed, Helen Henke, Unadilla, NE)

-18-

FAVORITE PUMPKIN COOKIES

1½ cups brown sugar, packed
1½ cups softened margarine
2 eggs
1 tsp. vanilla flavoring
1½ cups canned pumpkin
2¾ cups flour
4 tsp. baking powder
1 tsp. cinnamon
½ tsp. ginger
½ tsp. salt
¼ tsp. cloves
¼ tsp. nutmeg

Cream sugar, margarine, eggs and flavoring. Stir in pumpkin. Combine dry ingredients and add. Mix well. Drop by teaspoon on a greased cookie sheet. Bake at 375 degrees for 12 minutes or until done. Frost.

Frosting

2 Tbls. margarine, melted
⅓ cup pumpkin
1 tsp. vanilla flavoring
½ cup chopped pecans
Powdered sugar

Combine, using enough powdered sugar to make of spreading consistency. Spread on cooled cookies. (Honorable Mention--Veda Hilding, Shenandoah, IA)

DANISH PUFFS

1 cup flour
½ cup margarine
2 Tbls. water

Cut flour and margarine together with pastry blender. Add water and mix into a ball. Divide in two portions. Make two long strips (12x3-inches) and place on ungreased cookie sheet. Strips should be 3 inches apart. Prepare topping.

Puff Topping

½ cup margarine
1 tsp. almond flavoring
1 cup water
1 cup flour
3 eggs

Combine margarine, flavoring and water in pan and bring to a boil. Stir in flour all at once, mixing quickly. Beat in eggs with a spoon (not electric mixer) one at a time, beating until smooth each time. Spread half the puff mixture over each strip of pastry. Bake at 250 degrees about 50 minutes or until brown. Frost with powdered sugar icing and sprinkle with chopped nuts. Cut into bars or triangles. (Honorable Mention--Mary Chesshire, Shenandoah, IA)

-19-

TREASURES

1 cup softened margarine
1 cup peanut butter
2 tsp. vanilla flavoring
2 eggs
1 cup white sugar
1 cup brown sugar, packed
3 cups flour
1 tsp. baking powder
1 tsp. soda
½ tsp. salt
Miniature Milky Way or Three
  Musketeer candy bars

Cream margarine, peanut butter, flavoring, eggs and sugars together. Combine and add dry ingredients. Quarter tiny candy bars. Wrap enough dough around each piece just to cover. Bake on ungreased cookie sheet at 350 degrees just until set, about 8 minutes. Let cool on pan 5 minutes before removing. (A good way to use leftover Halloween candy.) (Honorable Mention--Mary Whitehill, Farragut, IA)

FRUIT CAKE BARS

6 Tbls. butter or margarine
4 cups vanilla wafer crumbs
¾ cup green candied cherries
½ cup candied pineapple
¾ cup chopped dates
1 cup whole pecans
1 can sweetened condensed milk
¼ cup bourbon

Melt butter or margarine in saucepan. Pour into a 10x13-inch pan. Sprinkle vanilla wafer crumbs over butter. Chop fruit and nuts and arrange evenly over crumbs. Press down gently. Combine the condensed milk and bourbon and pour over top. Bake at 350 degrees for 20 to 25 minutes. Remove from oven and cool completely. Cut into small squares or bars. (Honorable Mention--Mary Carse, Carson, IA)

CRISPY-MARSHMALLOW TREATS

½ cup butter or margarine
40 large marshmallows
6 cups crisp rice cereal

Melt butter or margarine; add marshmallows and stir until melted. Remove from heat and stir in cereal. Press into buttered 9x13-inch pan. Yield: 24 bars. (Honorable Mention-- Aaron Tebrinke, 7 years old, Red Oak, IA)

KMA 960

ARIZONA OATMEAL COOKIES

½ cup margarine
½ cup vegetable shortening
1 cup white sugar
½ cup brown sugar
1 egg
1 cup unsifted flour
1 tsp. soda
2 cups rolled oats
1 tsp. vanilla flavoring
½ cup chopped dates
6-oz. pkg. chocolate chips
½ cup chopped nuts

Cream shortenings and sugars together. Mix in egg and beat. Add flour and soda, then blend in rolled oats and flavoring. Divide dough into two parts. In one part put the dates, in other put chips and nuts. Drop by teaspoonsful on greased cookie sheets and bake at 375 degrees for about 10 minutes. A delightful way to make two kinds of cookies with one recipe. (Honorable Mention--Mrs. Paul Gerhardt, Mesa, AZ)

LEMONADE COOKIES

1 cup butter
1 cup sugar
2 eggs
3 cups sifted flour
1 tsp. soda
Dash of salt
½ cup frozen lemonade concentrate, undiluted
Sugar for top

Cream butter and sugar; beat in eggs. When light and fluffy, add dry ingredients which have been sifted together, alternating with ½ cup lemonade concentrate. Drop on ungreased cookie sheet. Brush with remaining lemonade concentrate and sprinkle with sugar. Bake about 8 minutes at 350 degrees. (Honorable Mention--Eldora McDougal, Lincoln, NE)

CHOCOLATE MACAROONS

14-oz. can sweetened condensed milk
4 1-oz. sq. unsweetened chocolate
¼ tsp. salt
1 tsp. vanilla flavoring
8 oz. shredded coconut
½ cup chopped nuts

Combine milk and chocolate in top of double boiler over hot, not boiling, water. Cook, stirring, until chocolate melts and mixture thickens--about 12 to 15 minutes. Remove from heat, add salt, flavoring, coconut and nuts. Mix well. Drop by rounded teaspoonsful on greased cookie sheets. Bake at 350 degrees about 10 minutes or just until set. Remove to wax paper to cool. (Honorable Mention--Mrs. Warren Miller, Randolph, IA)

SPECIAL STRAWBERRY DELIGHTS

5 Tbls. butter
2 eggs
1 cup sugar
¼ tsp. salt
1½ cup chopped dates
2½ cups crisp rice cereal
1 cup nuts
1 tsp. vanilla flavoring
Red-colored sugar
Green powdered sugar icing

Melt butter in fry pan (electric is best). Beat eggs, sugar and salt together and gradually stir into butter over low heat, watching carefully to prevent sticking. Add dates. Simmer gently, stirring, until mixture thickens. Cool slightly; add cereal, nuts and flavoring. Butter hands and shape mixture into small strawberries. Roll in red sugar. (Do not get too much on, just enough to make them red. You want to taste the filling, not the sugar.) For leaves, use green icing. The electric skillet is good to keep the mixture warm and pliable as you work with it. Pretty additions to a cookie tray. (Honorable Mention--Mrs. Ira Weppler, Lewis, IA)

FROSTED SQUARES

2¼ cups sifted flour
½ cup sugar
1 cup softened butter or margarine
2 eggs
1 cup brown sugar, packed
½ tsp. salt
1 tsp. baking powder
½ tsp. vanilla flavoring
3-oz. jar maraschino cherries
½ cup walnuts
½ cup flaked coconut

Combine flour, sugar and butter until crumbly. Press into 9x13-inch greased pan. Bake 15 minutes at 350 degrees. Blend eggs, brown sugar, salt, baking powder and flavoring. Drain cherries and chop, if desired, add. Stir in walnuts and coconut. Spoon over baked crust and bake 20 minutes longer. Frost.

Frosting

1 Tbls. butter
1 cup powdered sugar
Cherry juice
Coconut

Combine butter and sugar with just enough maraschino cherry juice to make of spreading consistency. Frost squares and sprinkle top with coconut. (Honorable Mention--Mabel Gilman, Earlham, IA)

UNBAKED BUTTER-PECAN GOODIES

2 cups white sugar
½ cup oil
6-oz. can evaporated milk
1 pkg. instant butterscotch pudding mix
3½ cups rolled oats

Combine first three ingredients in saucepan and bring to a good boil, stirring. Remove from heat; add remaining ingredients. Mix well. Cool 15 minutes and drop by teaspoon on wax paper. (Honorable Mention--Mrs. Bill Rhodes, Shenandoah, IA)

COOKIES ON A STICK

½ cup white sugar
½ cup brown sugar, packed
½ cup softened butter
¼ tsp. salt
1 beaten egg
1 tsp. vanilla flavoring
1 cup plus 2 Tbls. cake flour
½ tsp. soda
6-oz. pkg. chocolate chips
½ cup chopped peanuts
36 lollipop or ice cream sticks

Cream sugars and butter together. Beat in salt, egg and flavoring. Stir in flour and soda which have been sifted together. Add chips and nuts. Drop dough by rounded teaspoon on foil-lined cookie sheet. Space about 2 inches apart along two longer sides of sheet. (If dough is too sticky, put in freezer for a few minutes to firm.) Push a stick about two-thirds of the way into each ball of dough. Rest free end of stick on foil. Gently seal dough around stick. Chill in freezer for one more minute. Bake at 375 degrees for 8 to 10 minutes. Cool and wrap in plastic wrap. Tie with ribbon. Great for children's parties. (Honorable Mention--Jeff Erickson, Shenandoah, IA)

LITTLE BITTY LEMON COOKIES

1 Tbls. plus 2 tsp. margarine
2½ tsp. sugar
1½ tsp. fresh lemon juice
¼ tsp. grated lemon peel
⅓ cup plus 2 Tbls. cake flour

Using electric mixer, combine all ingredients with exception of flour; beat until light and smooth. Add flour and beat until mixture forms a sticky batter. Using wet hands, roll into 8 small balls. Arrange on non-stick baking sheet. With a fork, press each ball in checkerboard pattern. Bake at 300 degrees on lowest rack of oven about 15 minutes or until lightly browned. Remove to wire rack to cool. Yield: 8 cookies. (Honorable Mention--Carolyn Lothorp, Shenandoah, IA)

PETTICOAT TAILS

1 cup soft butter
1 cup sifted powdered sugar
1 tsp. flavoring (vanilla, almond, wintergreen or rose)
2½ cups sifted flour
¼ tsp. salt

Combine ingredients and mix well with hands. Shape into a 2-inch roll. Wrap in wax paper and chill until firm. Cut into thin slices and bake on ungreased cookie sheet at 400 degrees for 8 to 10 minutes or until light brown. Yield: 6 dozen. (Honorable Mention--Edna Ehlert, Woodbine, IA)

DATE KISSES

2 large egg whites
½ cup sugar
1 cup dates, quartered
4 large shredded wheat biscuits, crushed
1 tsp. vanilla flavoring
½ cup chopped pecans

Beat egg whites until stiff but not dry. Add sugar gradually as you continue beating. Lastly, fold in remaining ingredients. Drop from teaspoon on greased cookie sheets. Bake at 300 degrees about 30 minutes. Store in tight container. Yield: 2½ dozen. (Honorable Mention--Florence Nielson, Omaha, NE)

TRIX TREATS

12-oz. pkg. chocolate chips
½ cup butter (no substitute)
1 cup powdered sugar
3 cups Kix breakfast cereal
1 can sweetened condensed milk
1 cup small peanuts

Melt chocolate chips in top of double boiler, cool for a few minutes. Melt butter and add; stir in remaining ingredients. If sticky, chill for a few minutes. Roll into balls and place on wax paper. Can roll in coconut if desired. Kids love these. Yield: 150 small balls. (Honorable Mention--Vera Bredensteiner, Shenandoah, IA)

MY CHOCOLATE CHIP COOKIES

Make cookies. Push chocolate chips on top. Cook. (Honorable Mention--Lisa Tebrinke, Age 4, no town given.)

Through the years many of the prizewinning cookies from various fairs have found their way to the KMA Festivals. Also, a number of the KMA staff members have been judges at such events.

I have been a judge in the cookie department of the Iowa State Fair for five years. The following recipes are State Fair Winners including those identified as KMA WINNERS. Copies of KMA books were awarded to these contestants in honor of their excellence.

So, here are some of the Iowa State Fair winners, plus a few from county fairs–a sampling of those which have become part of the KMA Fall Festivals.

SWEEPSTAKES MARZIPAN BARS (KMA PRIZEWINNER)

1½ cup shortening
½ cup brown sugar
1 egg yolk
1 tsp. vanilla flavoring
½ tsp. baking soda
½ tsp. salt
2 cups flour
¼ cup milk
1 cup red raspberry jelly

Cream shortening and brown sugar. Beat in egg yolk and flavoring. Sift dry ingredients together and add with milk. Spread on bottom of greased jelly roll pan. Cover with jelly and make the following filling:

Almond Paste Filling

8-oz. can almond paste, cut in small pieces
1 egg white
1 tsp. vanilla flavoring
½ cup sugar
3 Tbls. shortening
3 eggs
Green food coloring

Blend first 5 ingredients. Add eggs one at a time and beat well. Tint a delicate green; pour over jelly layer. Bake at 350 degrees for 35 to 40 minutes. Cool. Frost with following icing.

Chocolate Icing

2 1-oz. sq. unsweetened chocolate, melted
1 Tbls. shortening
1 tsp. vanilla flavoring
2 cups powdered sugar
About ¼ cup hot milk

Combine all ingredients; beat until smooth. Stir in only enough milk to make of spreading consistency. Spread over top of almond layer and cut into bars. (Robin Tarbell, Centerville, IA)

BUTTERSCOTCH BARS

2 cups brown sugar, packed
½ cup butter
2 eggs
1 tsp. vanilla flavoring
2 cups flour
1 tsp. baking powder
¼ tsp. salt
1 cup coconut (or chocolate chips)
1 cup nuts

Cook brown sugar and butter over low heat until bubbly. Cool. Add eggs and flavoring. Sift in dry ingredients. Add coconut or chips and nuts. Spread in greased jelly roll pan; bake at 350 degrees for 25 minutes. Cut while warm. (Leona Ter Louw, Pella, IA)

CHRISTMAS PINWHEELS

½ cup butter
½ cup shortening
1 cup powdered sugar, sifted
1 egg
1½ tsp. almond flavoring
1 tsp. vanilla flavoring
2½ cups flour
1 tsp. salt
½ tsp. red food coloring
1 egg white, slightly beaten
½ cup crushed peppermints
½ cup sugar

Beat butter, shortening and powdered sugar together until light. Add egg and flavorings. Sift in flour and salt. Divide dough in two parts. Add red coloring to half. Cover and chill for an hour. Roll out white dough to 12-inch square. Repeat with red dough. Place red square on top of white. Roll to ¼-inch thickness. Roll up like jelly roll. Cover and chill again. Slice into ¼-inch thick circles; place on ungreased cookie sheets and bake at 375 degrees for 9 minutes or just until set. Do not overbake. Cool. Brush with egg white. Combine peppermints and remaining sugar and sprinkle over cookies. Yield: 6 dozen. (Sherry W. Snider, Des Moines, IA)

ROLLED SUGAR COOKIES

¾ cup shortening
1 cup sugar
2 eggs
¼ tsp. lemon flavoring
½ tsp. vanilla flavoring
2½ cups flour
1 tsp. baking powder
1 tsp. salt

Cream shortening and sugar, add eggs and flavorings. Sift in dry ingredients; mix well. Chill. Roll dough ¼-inch thick on floured board. Cut out and bake on ungreased cookie sheets at 400 degrees for 6 to 8 minutes. (Joy McFarland, Ellston, IA)

CHOCOLATE CHIP COOKIE
(KMA PRIZEWINNER)

1½ cup margarine
1 cup shortening
2 cups brown sugar, packed
2 cups white sugar
4 eggs
2 Tbls. vanilla flavoring
7 cups flour
1¼ Tbls. soda
¾ Tbls. salt
12-oz. pkg. chocolate chips

Cream margarine, shortening, sugars, eggs and flavoring until light and fluffy. Sift dry ingredients together and stir in. Add chips. Drop by teaspoonful onto greased cookie sheets. Bake at 350 degrees for 10 minutes. Yield: 14 dozen. (Darlys Orth, Ames, IA)

HOLIDAY RAISIN-PECAN BARS

1¼ cups flour
⅓ cup sugar
½ cup margarine
1 cup raisins
½ cup plum jam
2 eggs
¾ cup brown sugar, packed
¼ cup flour
¼ tsp. baking powder
¼ tsp. salt
1 cup chopped pecans
1 tsp. grated orange peel
1 tsp. vanilla flavoring

Combine 1¼ cups flour, sugar and margarine. Blend to fine crumbs. Press into bottom of greased 8-inch square pan. Bake at 350 degrees for 25 minutes (or until edges are light brown). Mix raisins and jam together. Spread over bottom layer. Beat eggs and brown sugar, add ¼ cup flour, baking powder and salt. Stir in rest of ingredients. Pour evenly over top of second layer. Bake 35 minutes or until top is brown and springs back when touched lightly in center. Cool in pan. Yield: 24. (Betty Link, Nevada, IA)

BLUE RIBBON FRUIT BARS

½ cup butter
¼ cup powdered sugar
1 cup flour
¼ tsp. salt
¾ tsp. almond flavoring
½ tsp. vanilla flavoring
1 tsp. apricot or peach flavoring
Apricot and/or pineapple preserves
Chopped red cherries and sliced
   almonds for garnish

Cream butter, powdered sugar, flour and salt. Add flavorings. Pat into ungreased 8x8-inch pan and bake at 350 degrees for 20 minutes. When cool, spread preserves over bars, then garnish with cherries and almonds. Cut into bars. (County Fair Winner)

SALTED NUT BARS (KMA PRIZEWINNER)

First Layer

3 cups sifted flour
1½ cups brown sugar, packed
1 cup butter or margarine, softened
½ tsp. salt

Combine ingredients; blend well. Press into ungreased jelly roll pan. Bake in 350 degree oven 10 to 12 minutes.

Second Layer

½ cup light corn syrup
2 Tbls. butter or margarine
1 Tbls. water
1 cup butterscotch chips
2 cups deluxe mixed nuts

In small saucepan combine all ingredients with the exception of the nuts. Boil for 2 minutes, stirring constantly. Sprinkle nuts over partially baked crust (nuts may be left whole or chopped). Pour butterscotch mixture over nuts. Return to oven and bake 10 to 12 minutes or until golden brown. Cool; cut into bars. (Betty Link, Nevada, IA)

DUFFY'S CHEWY CHOCOLATE BUTTER COOKIES

1¼ cups butter, softened
2 cups sugar
2 eggs
2 tsp. vanilla flavoring
2 cups flour
¾ cup cocoa
1 tsp. soda
½ tsp. salt
1 cup finely chopped nuts (optional)

Cream butter and sugar. Add eggs and flavoring and blend well. Combine dry ingredients and mix into creamed mixture. Stir in nuts. Drop by teaspoon onto an ungreased cookie sheet. Bake for 8 or 9 minutes in a 350 degree oven. The cookies puff up during baking, then flatten as they cool. Let cool on baking sheet at least 1 minute before removing. Yield: 5 dozen.

(Duffy Lyons is the lady who sculpts the life-size butter cow every year for the Iowa State Fair. No doubt she uses REAL butter when she makes these special cookies.)

CHOCOLATE DROP COOKIES

6 Tbls. shortening
¾ cup sugar
1½ envelopes unsweetened liquid
  chocolate
1 egg, well beaten
1 tsp. vanilla flavoring
1¼ cups flour
1 tsp. baking powder
½ tsp. soda
¼ tsp. salt
6 Tbls. milk

Cream shortening and sugar. Add chocolate, egg and flavoring. Mix well. Sift dry ingredients together. Add alternately with milk to first mixture. Beat well. Drop by rounded teaspoonsful onto baking sheets. Bake at 350 degrees for 10 minutes. When cool, frost with chocolate frosting. Yield: 1½ dozen. (Robin Tarbell, Centerville, IA)

CHOCOLATE-PEANUT BUTTER PINWHEELS

1 cup shortening
2 cups sugar
2 eggs
2 tsp. vanilla flavoring
3 cups flour
1 tsp. soda
1 tsp. salt
1-oz. sq. unsweetened chocolate
½ cup peanut butter

Cream shortening and sugar. Add eggs and flavoring; beat well. Blend in dry ingredients. Divide dough in half. Melt chocolate and mix in first half; add peanut butter to second. Divide in halves again. Roll each portion to 1/8-inch thick rectangle. Lay a chocolate dough piece on a peanut butter piece; roll jelly roll fashion; chill. Repeat (makes two rolls). Slice ½-inch thick, put on greased cookie sheet. Bake at 375 degrees for 10 to 12 minutes. Yield: 5 dozen. (Carole Miller, Altoona, IA)

HOLIDAY FRUIT DROPS

1 cup shortening
2 cups brown sugar
2 eggs
½ cup buttermilk
3½ cups flour
1 tsp. soda
1 tsp. salt
2 cups chopped candied cherries
2 cups chopped dates
1½ cups chopped pecans
Pecan halves

Cream shortening, sugar and eggs. Stir in buttermilk. Sift dry ingredients and add. Stir in fruits and nuts. Chill. Drop by rounded teaspoonsful on greased cookie sheet. Bake at 400 degrees for 8 to 10 minutes. Put a pecan half on top of each cookie. (Pat Hatch, West Des Moines, IA)

GRANOLA RASPBERRY BARS

1¼ cups flour
½ cup margarine
⅓ cup sugar
¾ cup raspberry preserves
½ cup raisins
½ cup milk chocolate bits
¼ cup honey
2 Tbls. margarine
¾ cup quick rolled oats
⅓ cup flaked coconut
⅓ cup sliced almonds
2 Tbls. sesame seeds

Put flour, the ½ cup margarine and sugar in mixer bowl and beat at low speed until crumbly. Press into greased 9x9-inch baking pan. Bake at 350 degrees for 15 to 20 minutes. Combine preserves, raisins and chocolate pieces; set aside. In heavy saucepan, combine honey and 2 Tbls. margarine. Heat and stir until melted. Add remaining ingredients and stir until blended. Spread preserve mixture over top of hot crust, then top with oat mixture; spread evenly to edge of pan. Bake 15 more minutes or until lightly browned. Cool; cut into bars. (Betty Link, Nevada, IA)

BUTTER PECAN CRISPS

1 cup butter
¾ cup white sugar
¾ cup brown sugar, packed
½ tsp. salt
2 eggs
1 tsp. vanilla flavoring
1½ cups finely ground pecans
2½ cups flour
1 tsp. soda
20 pecan halves, split lengthwise
4-oz. chocolate chips

Cream butter, sugars and salt. Beat in eggs, one at a time. Add flavoring and ground pecans. Combine flour and soda and add to batter. Drop by teaspoonsful on parchment lined cookie sheets. Top each with one pecan piece. Bake at 375 degrees for 9 to 12 minutes. When cool, melt chocolate chips and drizzle a zig-zag design over nut in center of each cookie. Yield: 4½ dozen. (Cynthia Weed, Indianola, IA)

MICROWAVE

MICROWAVE

This is the section which Ed May, Jr. requested. He and his wife Carolyn, like so many other young couples, are very busy people, and appreciate the convenience and speed of microwave cooking. Through the past few years more and more microwave cookies have surfaced at the KMA Fall Festivals, so they now have their own chapter.

CHOCOLATE CHIP COOKIES

1½ cup brown sugar, packed
½ cup softened margarine
1 egg
1 tsp. vanilla flavoring
½ cup flour
1 tsp. baking powder
Dash of salt
½ cup rolled oats
½ cup chocolate chips
½ cup chopped nuts

Cream sugar and margarine. Beat in egg and flavoring. Blend in dry ingredients. Stir in oats. Press into bottom of greased 8x8-inch round glass dish. Sprinkle with chips and nuts. Do not cover. Microwave on full power for 4 to 5 minutes. Cool. Cut into squares.

ALMOND-CHIP BARS

½ cup sugar
½ cup butter or margarine
1¼ cups flour
½ tsp. salt
1 tsp. vanilla flavoring
6-oz. chocolate chips
½ cup chopped almonds

Cream sugar and butter or margarine. Mix in flour, salt and flavoring. Press into greased and sugared 8x8-inch dish. Cover corners with foil. Cook 4 to 5 minutes on high; turn half-way through baking time. Remove foil, top with chips and return to oven for 1 more minute on high. Spread melted chips over top and sprinkle with nuts.

JIFFY MICROWAVE COOKIES

1 cup sugar
1 egg
1 tsp. soda
½ tsp. vanilla flavoring
1 cup creamy peanut butter

Beat sugar and egg together. Add remaining ingredients. Shape into balls and place on a paper plate covered with wax paper. Flatten with glass dipped in sugar. Bake only 8 cookies at a time for 2 to 2½ minutes at half power (50%). Rotate as needed. Yield: 3 dozen.

MADE-FROM-SCRATCH BARS

1½ cups butter
½ cup sugar
¼ cup chunky peanut butter
1 egg
1 tsp. vanilla flavoring
⅔ cup flour
½ tsp. baking powder
¼ tsp. salt
1 cup chocolate chips

Cream butter, sugar and peanut butter together. Add egg and flavoring and beat well. Stir in remaining ingredients. Spoon mixture into 8-inch square dish which has been lined with white paper towel. Microwave on half power (50%) for 7 minutes, then on high for 1 to 2 minutes or until top is just set, but not dry. Remove from microwave, cover with paper towel and let stand until cool.

Use only plain white paper towels and plates in the microwave. It is the ink on printed paper items which is undesirable when used with food.

CRISPY FUDGE LAYER BARS

½ cup peanut butter
¼ cup butter or margarine
4 cups small marshmallows
5 cups crisp rice cereal

Combine first three ingredients in glass bowl. Microwave on high for 1½ to 2 minutes, until melted--stir halfway through. Stir in crisp rice cereal. Put half cereal mixture into greased 9x9-inch pan. Spread on chocolate layer.

Chocolate Filling

1 cup chocolate chips
⅔ cup sweetened condensed milk
2 Tbls. butter or margarine

Combine in glass bowl and melt 1½ to 2 minutes on half power (50%). Stir. Spread on bottom layer and then top with rest of first crispy mixture. Chill.

BISCUIT MIX BARS

¾ cup chocolate chips
4 eggs
½ cup biscuit mix
½ cup brown sugar, packed
¼ cup melted butter or margarine
1 tsp. vanilla flavoring
¾ cup chopped peanuts

Melt chocolate for 1 minute on high. Stir once. Cool slightly. Beat in eggs; stir in remaining ingredients. Spoon into round baking dish which has been greased and sugared. Cook on high for 5 to 6 minutes, turning once.

PEANUTTY BARS
(With Microwave Topping)

1½ cups flour
⅔ cup brown sugar, packed
¼ tsp. baking powder
⅓ tsp. salt
¼ tsp. soda
1 tsp. vanilla flavoring
½ cup margarine
2 egg yolks

Combine ingredients, mix well, and press into greased 9x13-inch dish. Bake in 325 degree oven 12 to 15 minutes. Remove and cover with small marshmallows. Microwave 1 minute. Cool. Cover with the following topping.

Peanut Butter Topping

12-oz. pkg. peanut butter chips
2 tsp. vanilla flavoring
¼ cup margarine
⅔ cup corn syrup
2 cups crisp rice cereal

Combine first four ingredients in glass bowl. Microwave on high for 1 to 2 minutes or until melted, stirring once. Fold in crisp rice cereal and spread over marshmallow layer.

CHOCOLATE CIRCLE

Favorite sugar cookie recipe
  (or refrigerated cookie roll)
⅔ cup peanut butter
½ cup chocolate chips
⅔ cup sweetened condensed milk
½ tsp. vanilla flavoring
½ tsp. burnt sugar flavoring
½ cup peanuts (optional)

Pat cookie dough in round greased microwave dish until about ⅓-inch thick. Combine peanut butter, chocolate chips and milk in glass bowl and melt for 1 to 2 minutes on high, stirring at least once. Add flavorings and spread over cookie circle. Sprinkle with finely chopped peanuts. Bake at half power (50%) for 6 minutes or until barely done, turning once. Let stand 5 minutes before cutting.

ALMOND BARK COOKIES

2 lbs. almond bark
1 cup peanut butter
2 cups tiny marshmallows
1 to 2 cups peanuts
3 cups crisp rice cereal

Melt bark in microwave dish on high for about 2 minutes, stirring once, until melted. Stir in remaining ingredients. Drop by spoonsful on wax paper. Let set.

MICROWAVE GRANOLA BARS

2 cups granola
1 egg, beaten
½ cup chopped dates
½ cup chopped dried apricots
½ cup peanuts
¼ cup brown sugar, packed
½ tsp. vanilla flavoring

Mix all ingredients together. Line 8-inch round dish with wax paper. Press mixture into dish. Cook, uncovered, on high for 3½ minutes or until set. Turn halfway through cooking. Cool, then remove from pan, peel off wax paper and cut into bars.

❖━━━━━━❖

FILLED FUDGIES

½ cup peanut butter
6-oz. pkg. butterscotch chips
4 cups crisp rice cereal
6-oz. pkg. chocolate chips
½ cup powdered sugar
2 Tbls. butter or margarine
1 tsp. vanilla flavoring
1 Tbls. water

Put peanut butter and butterscotch chips into glass bowl or large measuring cup and melt at medium (50%) power for 2 minutes, stirring once during cooking. Stir in rice cereal and press half the mixture into an 8x8-inch greased dish. Combine remaining ingredients and cook at medium (50%) power for about 2½ minutes or until melted and smooth. Stir once or twice. Spread over first layer and top with remaining cereal mixture. Chill if needed and cut.

❖━━━━━━❖

Do not grease and flour microwave dishes and pans for baking; the batter will stick. Grease and sprinkle with sugar.

❖━━━━━━❖

BLONDE-CHIP BARS

½ cup butter or margarine
¾ cup brown sugar, packed
2 eggs
1 tsp. vanilla flavoring
¼ tsp. baking powder
¾ cup flour
¼ tsp. salt
½ cup chocolate chips
½ cup nuts

Combine butter or margarine and brown sugar in microwave bowl and melt for 1 minute on high. Stir and add eggs and flavoring. Sift in dry ingredients. Add chips and nuts. Spread into a greased and sugared 8-inch round glass dish. Cook for 4 minutes on high, rotating once; cook for another 1 minute, or until barely done-still should be moist on top.

FIVE LAYER MICROWAVE BARS

4 Tbls. butter or margarine
1 cup graham cracker crumbs
6-oz. pkg. chocolate chips
6-oz. pkg. butterscotch chips
3½-oz. can flaked coconut
½ cup chopped walnuts
15-oz. can sweetened condensed milk

Put butter or margarine in 9x12-inch glass dish and melt on high power for about 45 seconds. Tilt dish to spread around. Place an inverted 2½-inch glass in center. Sprinkle crumbs evenly over butter. Layer chocolate, butterscotch chips, coconut and nuts on top of crumbs. Pour sweetened condensed milk over all. Bake, uncovered, on high for 6 minutes. Turn dish half a turn after 3 minutes. Cool, cut into bars.

COCOA BROWNIES

⅓ cup cocoa
½ cup butter or margarine
1 cup sugar
2 eggs
1 tsp. vanilla flavoring
1 tsp. burnt sugar flavoring
¾ cup flour
½ tsp. baking powder
A dash of salt

Melt cocoa and butter or margarine together in glass bowl for 1 minute on high. Add sugar. Blend in eggs and flavorings. Add dry ingredients. Spoon into buttered and sugared 8x8-inch square dish. Cover corners with foil. Bake on high for 4 minutes. Remove foil and cook for 2 more minutes, or until top is just barely dry. Do not overbake. Frost if desired.

MICROWAVE FROSTING

¼ cup butter or margarine
3-oz. pkg. cream cheese
2 cups powdered sugar
½ tsp. vanilla flavoring
½ tsp. almond flavoring

Combine in glass bowl. Microwave 30 seconds on high, or until ingredients are soft. Beat well. Frost bars or cookies, those made in microwave or in regular oven.

QUICKY BARS

6-oz. pkg. chocolate chips
6-oz. pkg. butterscotch chips
½ cup margarine
¾ cup peanut butter
2 cups miniature marshmallows
½ to 1 cup peanuts

Combine chips, margarine and peanut butter in microwave dish. Melt, on high for 2 minutes. Stir. Add marshmallows and peanuts. Chill.

APRICOT TREATS

1½ cups rolled oats
1½ cups flour
Dash of salt
1 tsp. baking powder
1 cup brown sugar, packed
⅔ cup softened butter or margarine
½ tsp. burnt sugar flavoring
½ tsp. almond flavoring
½ cup apricot preserves

Combine dry ingredients. Cut in butter and flavorings until crumbly. Butter and sugar 8-inch round pyrex dish. Spoon half crumbly mixture into pan and pat firm. Microwave at 70% (medium high) for 4 minutes, turn once. Spread preserves over layer and sprinkle remaining crumb mixture on top, pressing down gently. Microwave 4 minutes at 70%. Cool before cutting.

RAISIN BARS

¼ cup melted margarine
⅔ cup brown sugar, packed
1 egg, beaten
1 cup unsweetened applesauce
1 cup flour
½ tsp. soda
½ tsp. cinnamon
¼ tsp. salt
¼ tsp. nutmeg
1/8 tsp. ground cloves
½ cup raisins

Grease an 8x12-inch microwave dish. Sprinkle some sugar and cinnamon on bottom. Spoon margarine on top. Microwave, uncovered, for 20 seconds. Combine sugar, egg and applesauce. Add dry ingredients which have been sifted together. When smooth, stir in raisins. Spread evenly in baking dish. Microwave at 70% for 9 minutes. Turn once. Sprinkle with powdered sugar.

GRAHAM CEREAL BARS

3 Tbls. milk
14 caramels
6-oz. pkg. butterscotch chips
½ tsp. vanilla flavoring
4 cups graham cereal
½ cup peanuts

Melt milk and caramels together in bowl for 2 minutes on high. Stir at least once as mixure melts. Add half butterscotch pieces and stir until melted. Stir in remaining ingredients and spoon into greased 8-inch square pan. Melt remaining chips on high, for 1 minute, or until soft. Stir and use to frost bars.

Cookies

If your microwave can take foil, cover corners of square dishes with triangles of foil to keep from over-baking that area of bar cookies and cakes.

CHERRY DELIGHT WEDGES

1 can cherry pie filling
½ tsp. almond flavoring
1 small (9-oz.) box white cake mix
3 Tbls. butter or margarine
⅔ cup brown sugar
½ cup chopped nuts

Combine pie filling and flavoring. Combine remaining ingredients to make a crumbly mixture. Spread half in bottom of 8-inch round pyrex dish which has been buttered and sugared. Spoon cherry mixture over first layer, then top with rest of crumb mixture and pat down gently. Microwave on high for 9 to 10 minutes. Turn once or twice during cooking time to bake evenly. Cool before cutting.

Microwaves keep cooking inside the food after it is removed from the oven. During the 'resting time' after they come from the oven they are still baking.

ALMOND BARK COOKIE

3 cups flour
1 cup lard
1 egg
1 tsp. vinegar
5 Tbls. water
1 tsp. salt
Pinch baking powder

Cut flour and lard together. Beat remaining ingredients together and add. Roll into a ball. Roll out on lightly floured board; use half for bottom and half for top. (Use deep dish round or 8-inch square pan.)

Filling

1½ cups sugar
2 eggs
6 Tbls. flour
8 Tbls. milk
4 tsp. almond flavoring

Combine all ingredients in glass bowl and microwave until boiling on high, stirring once. Pour filling into bottom crust and top with remaining crust. Microwave on medium for 12 to 15 minutes--put dish up on an inverted glass pie plate to circulate microwaves underneath to cook bottom crust--then brown in a toaster oven or a conventional oven. (Can bake in conventional oven for 30 to 35 minutes at 375 degrees, until brown.)

CREME DE MENTHE BARS

First Layer

2 1-oz. sq. unsweetened chocolate
½ cup butter or margarine
½ cup white sugar
½ cup brown sugar, packed
2 eggs
1 tsp. vanilla flavoring
⅔ cup flour
A dash of salt
½ tsp. baking powder

Put chocolate and butter in glass bowl and microwave 1 to 2 minutes on high (100% power) or until melted. Stir. Blend in sugars; beat in eggs one at a time. Stir in rest of ingredients and spread into a 9 x 13-inch glass baking dish. If microwave can take foil, cover corners with triangles of foil. Cover with plastic wrap and microwave on high for 5 to 6 minutes, turn half-way around once. Cool.

Middle Layer

½ cup butter or margarine
2 cups powdered sugar
2 Tbls. creme de menthe
1/8 tsp. green food coloring
½ tsp. mint flavoring

Put butter in bowl and microwave on high 20 seconds to soften. Mix in powdered sugar and beat well. Add remaining ingredients and beat until smooth and fluffy. Spread evenly over cooled first layer. Refrigerate.

Topping

6-oz. chocolate chips
2 Tbls. oil
½ tsp. vanilla flavoring

Combine ingredients in bowl and microwave on high for 1 to 1½ minutes. Stir until smooth. Spread over middle layer. Store in refrigerator until time to serve.

◈══════════◈

TURTLES

Turtles can be sneaky and these got into the KMA Festival.

Pecan halves
14-oz. pkg. caramels
12-oz. chocolate chips

Butter microwave plate. Arrange pecan halves in 6 groups of three. Unwrap 6 caramels and put one on top of each cluster of pecans. Microwave at lowest power for 3 to 4 minutes-- just until caramels are soft enough to press down with back of spoon. Repeat. When all the caramel-nut shapes are done, microwave chips in glass bowl for 1½ to 2 minutes; stir until smooth. Put a little chocolate on top of each caramel to make a turtle.

DIET:
Sugarless
Low-Calorie
Healthy

DIET

Cooking has changed through the years and this is definitely apparent in cookie making. More and more of the recipes brought to the KMA Fall Festivals are low-calorie, use less sugar and have nutritious combinations of ingredients. People are healthier and so are the cookies they are making.

LOW-CALORIE DELIGHTS

1 cup plus 2 Tbls. flour
¼ tsp. baking powder
1/8 tsp. salt
¼ cup margarine
¼ cup sugar
1 egg
¾ tsp. vanilla flavoring
½ tsp. pineapple flavoring
8-oz. can crushed pineapple, drained
4 packets Sweet 'N Low or the
    equivalent in liquid sweetener

Sift dry ingredients together. In separate bowl, cream margarine and sugar. Add egg, flavoring, pineapple and sweetener. Beat well. Stir in dry ingredients. Chill. Bake on non-stick cookie sheet. Shape dough into small balls. Press flat with bottom of floured glass. Make design with fork. Bake 6 to 8 minutes at 400 degrees. Yield: 2½ dozen at 35 calories each.

SUGARLESS RAISIN COOKIES

1 cup water
1 cup chopped raisins
2 cups chopped apples
¼ cup shortening
1 tsp. cinnamon
¼ tsp. nutmeg
2 tsp. liquid sweetener
1 egg
1 tsp. vanilla flavoring
1 cup flour
1 tsp. soda
¼ tsp. salt
½ cup nuts

Combine first 6 items and boil for 5 minutes. Remove from heat and add sweetener. Cool. Beat in egg and flavoring. Sift dry ingredients together and add. Stir in nuts. Drop by teaspoon on greased cookie sheet. Bake at 350 degrees for 8 to 10 minutes.

NUT CRUNCHIES

1 Tbls. fruit juice
4 eggs
¼ tsp. almond flavoring
2/3 cup flour
1/3 tsp. soda
2 cups ground nuts

Beat fruit juice and eggs together. Mix in rest of ingredients. Drop by teaspoonsful on greased cookie sheet. Bake at 375 degrees for about 6 minutes.

FRUCTOSE FANCIES

6 Tbls. margarine, softened
½ cup fructose
¼ cup liquid egg substitute
  (or 1 egg)
1 tsp. vanilla flavoring
2 cups flour
Dash of salt
2 tsp. baking powder

Combine margarine and fructose and beat until smooth. Add egg substitute (or egg) and flavoring. Beat in dry ingredients. Drop by teaspoonsful on greased cookie sheet. Bake at 400 degrees for 8 to 10 minutes. (Can make into rolled out cookies by chilling well, then roll and cut.)

BANANA-PINEAPPLE DELIGHTS

1 cup flour
⅓ tsp. soda
¼ cup mashed bananas
¼ cup frozen pineapple juice,
  undiluted
¼ cup cooking oil
¼ tsp. pineapple flavoring
1 egg
½ cup coconut
1 Tbls. milk (if needed)

Combine flour and soda. Beat bananas, juice, oil, flavoring and egg together. Fold in flour and coconut (add milk if needed to make of dropping consistency). Drop on greased cookie sheet and top each cookie with a bit of coconut. Bake at 350 degrees for 8 to 10 minutes. Yield 30.

CLASSY DATE SANDWICHES

1 cup chopped dates
¾ cup water
1 cup flour
½ tsp. soda
Dash salt
⅓ cup shortening
3 Tbls. fruit juice

Combine dates and water and simmer, stirring occasionally, until thick. Cool. Mix together the flour, soda and salt. Cut in shortening. Gently stir in fruit juice of your choice until mixture forms into a ball. Roll out on lightly floured board and cut into rounds; place on greased cookie sheet. Prick with fork. Bake at 375 degrees until light brown. Put together like sandwiches with date filling. Cool.

LOW-CHOLESTEROL COOKIE

1 cup flour
½ tsp. soda
1 tsp. salt
¼ tsp. cinnamon
1½ cups rolled oats
2 egg whites
1 cup brown sugar, packed
⅓ cup cooking oil
½ cup skim milk
1 tsp. vanilla flavoring
1 cup raisins

Sift flour, soda, salt and cinnamon together. Stir into oats. Beat egg whites with a fork and then combine with sugar, oil, milk, flavoring and raisins. Lastly, combine with flour mixture. Mix well. Drop batter a teaspoon at a time on oiled cookie sheet. Bake 12 to 15 minutes. (Shorter baking time makes for a chewy cookie; bake longer and they are crisp.) Yield: 3 dozen.

SUGARLESS FRUIT DELIGHTS

½ cup prunes
½ cup raisins
½ cup dates
½ cup water
½ cup margarine
1 cup flour
1 tsp. cinnamon
1 tsp. vanilla flavoring
1 tsp. soda
1 egg
½ cup chopped nuts

Cook fruit in water for 6 minutes. Add margarine and cool. Mix in remaining ingredients. Drop on greased cookie sheet and bake at 350 degrees for 10 to 12 minutes. Yield: 3 dozen cookies at 53 calories each.

LOW-CAL CHOCOLATE CHIP DROPS

¼ cup light corn syrup
¼ cup brown sugar, packed
1 Tbls. vegetable shortening
2 egg whites, stiffly beaten
2 Tbls. water
½ tsp. vanilla flavoring
⅔ cup flour
½ cup nonfat dry milk
½ tsp. soda
½ tsp. salt
1½ cups quick rolled oats
2 Tbls. all-bran cereal
½ cup chocolate chips

Cream syrup, sugar and shortening with electric mixer until smooth and creamy. Add stiffly beaten egg whites, water and flavoring. Mix on medium speed for 1 minute. Add flour, dry milk, soda and salt. Mix on low speed for 2 minutes until thick and fluffy. Stir in cereals and chips. Drop by teaspoon on greased cookie sheet and bake at 375 degrees for about 10 minutes, or until done.

DIABETIC LEMON COOKIE

½ cup vegetable shortening
¼ tsp. butter flavoring
2 Tbls. liquid sweetener
1 egg
1 Tbls. water
1 tsp. lemon flavoring
1 Tbls. lemon juice
1⅔ cups sifted cake flour
1 tsp. baking powder
½ cup chopped nuts

Cream shortening and butter flavoring with sweetener. Beat in egg, water, lemon flavoring and juice. Sift flour and baking powder into creamed mixture. Add nuts. Form into rolls and wrap in foil. Chill well. Slice and bake on greased cookie sheets for 10 minutes in a 400 degree oven. (These do not brown like cookies made with sugar; check for doneness by texture.)

NO-SUGAR COOKIE

½ cup soft margarine
2 tsp. vanilla flavoring
1 egg
1 cup flour
1 tsp. baking powder
Dash of salt
1 cup chopped dates
1 cup chopped nuts
1 cup shredded coconut

Cream margarine, flavoring and egg together. Combine flour, baking pow-
der and salt and blend into creamed mixture. Stir in remaining ingredients. Form into rolls. Wrap in wax paper and chill well. (Can be frozen up to 4 weeks.) When ready to use, slice and place on greased cookie sheet and bake at 350 degrees for 8 to 10 minutes.

SUNFLOWER COOKIES

2 cups whole wheat flour
1 tsp. cinnamon
½ tsp. salt
½ cup mashed bananas
⅔ cup peanut butter
⅔ cup molasses or sorghum
1 egg, beaten
1 cup sunflower seeds

Combine dry ingredients, set aside. Cream bananas, peanut butter, molasses and egg together; blend in dry ingredients. Fold in sunflower seeds--chop seeds if you want finer pieces. Drop by teaspoonful on greased cookie sheet. Bake at 350 degrees about 10 minutes. Yield: 3 dozen.

"CHOCOLATE" CAROB COOKIES

1 ¾ cups flour
1 ½ tsp. baking powder
½ cup carob powder
½ cup honey
½ cup shortening
1 egg
1 tsp. vanilla flavoring
¼ tsp. burnt sugar flavoring
½ cup milk
½ cup raisins
½ cup nuts

Sift dry ingredients together. Mix next 5 ingredients. Add dry mixture and milk alternately; stir in raisins and nuts. Drop by teaspoon on greased cookie sheet. Bake 8 to 10 minutes at 350 degrees.

NO-BAKE CAROB NUT ROLL

½ cup soft margarine
6 Tbls. honey
2 Tbls. molasses
½ cup carob powder
¾ cup nonfat dry milk
½ cup chopped English walnuts
¼ cup ground English walnuts

Cream margarine with honey and molasses. Beat in carob powder. Gradually beat in the dry milk until mixture is stiff enough to hold a shape. Add chopped walnuts and form into an 8-inch roll about ½ inch in diameter. Coat with ground walnuts. Chill.

CRISPY RAISIN DROPS

½ cup butter or margarine
½ cup brown sugar, packed
¼ cup white sugar
1 egg
½ tsp. vanilla flavoring
1 cup flour
½ tsp. salt
½ tsp. soda
½ cup granola
½ cup carob covered raisins

Cream butter and sugars. Beat in egg and flavoring. Combine dry ingredients and stir in. Add granola and raisins. Drop by heaping teaspoons on greased baking sheet. Bake at 375 degrees for 10 minutes.

SUGARLESS FRUIT BARS

1 cup flour
Dash salt
⅓ cup butter
1 cup chopped dried fruit
¾ cup water
¼ tsp. almond flavoring

Combine flour and salt; cut in butter. Pat mixture into bottom of 8-inch square greased baking pan. Bake at 350 degrees for 12 minutes. Combine fruit (chopped dates, figs, dried apricots, etc.) with water and flavoring and cook until thick. Spread over crust and return to oven to bake for 12 to 15 more minutes.

BRAN YO-YOS

1 cup butter or margarine
1½ cups brown sugar, packed
2 eggs
1 tsp. water
½ tsp. vanilla flavoring
½ tsp. burnt sugar flavoring
1 cup bran cereal
2 cups whole wheat flour
1 tsp. baking powder
½ tsp. salt
1 cup nuts
1 cup chocolate or carob chips

Cream butter and sugar together. Beat in eggs, water and flavorings. Blend well. Add cereal. Let stand several minutes. Combine dry ingredients, stir in. Add nuts and chips. Drop by teaspoon onto greased cookie sheet and bake about 10 minutes at 350 degrees. Yield: 10 dozen.

UNBAKED GRANOLA BALLS

½ cup butter or margarine
⅓ cup honey
2 cups chopped dates
2 cups granola
2 cups nuts or coconut for coating

Melt butter or margarine. Add honey and dates and cook until dates are soft. Remove from heat and stir In granola. When cool, roll into balls and then coat with chopped nuts or coconut. Keep in refrigerator until time to serve.

GRANOLA

3 cups rolled oats
½ cup cooking oil
1 cup sesame seeds
1½ cups wheat germ
1½ cups unsweetened coconut
1 cup chopped nuts
½ to 1 cup honey (optional)
1 cup dried fruits (optional)

Combine all ingredients. For sugarless, do not put in honey but add 1 cup dried, chopped fruit. Toast in 275 degree oven for about 30 minutes, stirring often. Store in can with tight lid.

WHOLE WHEAT GOODIES

1 cup molasses or sorghum
1 cup apple juice
⅔ cup cooking oil
2½ cups whole wheat flour
1 tsp. cinnamon
¼ tsp. nutmeg
¼ tsp. cloves
¼ tsp. salt
1 cup sunflower seeds
2½ cups diced apple
3 cups rolled oats

Combine first three ingredients. Mix dry ingredients together and add to first mixture. Fold in remaining ingredients. Drop by tablespoon onto greased cookie sheet. Bake at 350 degrees for 13 minutes or until done. Yield: 4 dozen.

BRAN DROP COOKIES

½ cup butter or shortening
¾ cup brown sugar, packed
2 eggs, beaten
½ tsp. almond flavoring
½ tsp. vanilla flavoring
1½ cups flour
2 tsp. baking powder
¼ tsp. salt
1 cup chopped nuts
1 cup raisins or dates
1 cup whole bran

Cream butter, add sugar and beat well. Stir in eggs. Sift in dry ingredients and add nuts, dates and bran. Drop on greased baking sheet. Bake at 400 degrees for about 10 minutes.

UNSWEET PEANUT BUTTERS

½ cup peanut butter
2 eggs
½ tsp. vanilla flavoring
¼ cup mashed bananas
2 Tbls. softened butter
1 cup flour
½ tsp. baking powder
½ tsp. mace or cinnamon
1 cup chopped peanuts

Beat together the peanut butter and eggs. Mix in flavoring, bananas and butter. Combine remaining ingredients and mix in. Drop by teaspoonsful on greased cookie sheet. Bake at 375 degrees for 6 or 7 minutes.

APPLESAUCE BARS

1 cup applesauce
3 eggs
¼ cup butter
½ tsp. vanilla flavoring
2 cups flour
1 tsp. soda
2 tsp. baking powder
1 tsp. cinnamon
1 cup raisins

For completely sugar-free bars, use unsweetened applesauce. Combine applesauce, eggs, butter and flavoring and beat well. Stir in remaining ingredients and spoon into greased 8-inch square baking pan. Bake at 350 degrees for 25 minutes, until firm.

WHEAT GERM BARS

½ cup butter or margarine
½ cup brown sugar, packed
1 egg
1 tsp. vanilla flavoring
¾ cup wheat germ
½ cup whole wheat flour
¼ tsp. soda
½ cup chopped peanuts

Mix ingredients well in order given. Press into greased 9x13-inch baking pan. Bake at 325 degrees for about 20 minutes or until light brown. Cool and cut.

DIABETIC COOKIES

1¼ cups water
⅓ cup margarine
2 cups raisins
2 tsp. cinnamon
2 eggs, beaten
2 Tbls. water
¼ tsp. soda
3 Tbls. liquid sweetener
1 tsp. vanilla flavoring
2 cups flour
1 Tbls. baking powder

Combine 1¼ cups water, margarine and raisins in a pan and boil 3 minutes. Remove from fire, stir in cinnamon. Beat in eggs, water, salt, soda, sweetener and flavoring. Mix flour and baking powder together and stir in. Drop by teaspoon on greased cookie sheet. Bake at 325 degrees for 10 to 12 minutes.

━━━━━━━━━━

WHOLE WHEAT PEANUT COOKIES

1 cup brown sugar, packed
¾ cup margarine
1 egg
1 cup whole wheat flour
¼ cup wheat germ
2 tsp. baking powder
¼ cup nonfat dry milk
1¾ cups rolled oats
½ cup raisins
12-oz. pkg. peanut butter chips
   (optional)

Beat sugar, margarine and egg together. Combine dry ingredients and blend in. Add rest of ingredients. Dough is very stiff. Drop on greased baking sheet. Bake at 350 degrees for 12 to 14 minutes. Cool slightly before removing from the rack.

BRAN-BANANA DROPS

1 cup whole bran cereal
6 Tbls. sugar
½ tsp. cinnamon
1 cup sugar
½ cup shortening
¼ cup butter
2 eggs
1½ tsp. vanilla flavoring
1 cup mashed bananas
2½ cups flour
3 tsp. baking powder
½ tsp. salt

Place bran cereal on sheet of wax paper and roll fine with rolling pin. Add 6 Tbls. sugar and cinnamon; mix. Set aside. Beat 1 cup sugar, shortening, and butter until light and fluffy. Beat in eggs and flavoring. Stir in bananas. Sift dry ingredients together and stir into creamed mixture. Drop by teaspoonsful into bran mixture and turn to coat. Place on greased baking sheet. Bake at 400 degrees for 10 minutes. Frost, if desired.

CRUNCHY WHOLE GRAIN COOKIES

½ cup shortening
1 cup sugar
2 eggs
1 tsp. vanilla flavoring
¼ tsp. salt
2 tsp. water
½ tsp. soda
2 cups flour
½ tsp. cinnamon
¼ tsp. cloves
¼ tsp. nutmeg
2 cups whole grain wheat flakes
1 cup raisins

Cream shortening and sugar; beat in eggs, flavoring and salt. Dissolve soda in water. Stir in. Lastly, add dry ingredients, flakes and raisins. Drop by teaspoon on greased cookie sheet. Bake at 375 degrees for 10 minutes.

HONEY BRAN COOKIES

½ cup sugar
½ cup honey
½ cup butter
1 tsp. maple flavoring
2 Tbls. milk
1½ cups flour
½ tsp. soda
¼ tsp. salt
½ tsp. cinnamon
1½ cups raisin bran
¼ cup raisins

Mix ingredients in order given. Blend well. Drop on greased cookie sheet and bake at 350 degrees until brown--about 10 minutes.

HIGH ENERGY COOKIES

1 cup raisins
½ cup water
1 cup shortening
½ cup white sugar
½ cup brown sugar, packed
½ cup peanut butter
2 eggs
1 tsp. vanilla flavoring
2 cups flour
1 tsp. soda
½ tsp. salt
½ tsp. cinnamon
¼ tsp. nutmeg
1½ cups rolled oats
½ cup wheat germ
½ cups nuts
½ cup sunflower seeds

Cook raisins in water until tender. Reserve 5 Tbls. liquid. Cream shortening, sugars and peanut butter. Beat in eggs and flavoring. Combine dry ingredients and stir in alternately with raisin water. Add everything else. Drop by spoonful on greased cookie sheet. Bake for about 10 minutes at 375 degrees.

WHOLE WHEAT-OATMEAL DROPS

1 cup raisins
Water
1 cup shortening
¾ cup white sugar
¾ cup brown sugar, packed
2 eggs
1 cup whole wheat flour
1 cup white flour
½ tsp. salt
½ tsp. soda
1 tsp. cinnamon
2 cups rolled oats
½ cup nuts

Cover raisins with water and bring to boil. Remove from heat, cover, cool, drain and grind. Cream shortening and sugars until light. Beat in eggs. Stir dry ingredients together and add to creamed mixture. Stir in rest. Drop by teaspoon onto greased cookie sheet. Bake at 350 degrees for 10 to 12 minutes. Cool on cookie sheet 2 minutes, then remove to racks.

WHEAT GRANOLA BARS

¾ cup margarine
⅓ cup brown sugar, packed
2 Tbls. honey
1 beaten egg
3 cups finely crushed shredded
    wheat biscuits
¾ cups chopped peanuts
1 cup steamed raisins

In large saucepan, melt margarine, sugar and honey. Remove from heat and cool 5 minutes. Add remaining ingredients in order given. Press into greased 9x13-inch pan. Bake at 350 degrees for 25 minutes. Cut while warm.

DAVY CROCKETT BARS

1 cup white sugar
1 cup brown sugar, packed
½ cup margarine
½ cup shortening
2 eggs
1 tsp. vanilla flavoring
½ tsp. burnt sugar flavoring
2 cups flour
1 tsp. soda
½ tsp. salt
1 tsp. baking powder
2 cups rolled oats
1 cup chocolate chips
½ cup coconut
½ cup raisins
¼ cup wheat germ
½ cup chopped apples
¼ cup sunflower seed

Mix first seven ingredients until smooth and fluffy. Mix in combined dry ingredients. Stir in rest. Spread in greased jelly roll pan. Bake at 350 degrees for 30 minutes or until done. When cool, cut into bars. Frost if desired.

CAREFREE:
Made-From-Mixes
Processor
Unbaked

CAREFREE

Carefree cookies, what a great picture those words bring to mind. Today the homemaker has many types of mixes--cake, biscuit, pudding and a variety of pie fillings--at hand to help make cooking easier. Or, as some of our Festival folks have shown us, you can make your own mix.

Kitchen equipment which helps in preparation by chopping, stirring and whipping ingredients help cookie making become especially simple.

And the unbaked cookies go together fast and are sweet and good.

Carefree cookies, what a marvelous idea!

COOKIE MIX BROWNIES

2 cups homemade mix
2 1-oz. sq. unsweetened chocolate, melted
2 eggs
½ cup brown sugar, packed
¼ cup water
1 tsp. vanilla flavoring
Nuts (optional)

Combine ingredients. Spread in greased and floured 9-inch square pan. Bake at 350 degrees for 25 minutes. Yield: 2 dozen.

YOUR OWN COOKIE MIX

9 cups flour
3 cups nonfat dry milk
1 Tbls. salt
3 Tbls. baking powder
4 cups homogenized shortening
4 cup sugar

Combine dry ingredients--mix well. Cream shortening and sugar; cut into dry ingredients. Mixture will be crumbly. Store in covered container, preferably in refrigerator. Will keep several weeks. Spoon mix lightly into cup to measure for cookies.

COOKIE MIX SUGAR COOKIES

3 cups cookie mix
1 egg
½ tsp. vanilla flavoring
½ tsp. almond flavoring

Combine ingredients. Add a little water, if needed. Chill dough. Roll and cut, drop or shape as desired. Put on greased baking sheet. Sprinkle with sugar. Bake at 375 degrees for 8 minutes.

CHERRY PIE MIX BARS

1 cup margarine
1⅓ cups sugar
4 eggs
1 tsp. vanilla flavoring
1½ tsp. baking powder
3 cups flour
1 can cherry pie filling

Cream margarine and sugar. Add one egg at a time, beating well after each, then stir in flavoring, baking powder and flour. Spread ⅔ of batter in greased jelly roll pan. Spread pie filling on top of dough. Drop remainder of batter by teaspoonful over the pie filling. Smooth out a little. Bake at 350 degrees for 35 to 40 minutes. Frost while still warm with powdered sugar icing flavored with almond flavoring.

RUBY'S QUICK BARS

1 regular-size yellow cake mix
2 eggs
1 tsp. orange flavoring
1¼ cups 7-Up
1 cup chopped nuts

Combine and beat well. Spread onto greased jelly roll pan. Sprinkle top with nuts, if desired. Bake at 350 degrees for 15 minutes or until done. Cut into bars. Yield: 60. Freeze well.

PANCAKE MIX COOKIES

1 cup prepared pancake mix
¾ cup brown sugar, packed
½ cup soft shortening
½ cup peanut butter
1 egg
1 tsp. vanilla flavoring
1½ cup rolled oats

Combine all ingredients with exception of rolled oats and beat for 2 minutes with electric mixer. Stir in oats. Chill dough, roll into balls and place on greased cookie sheet. Flatten with greased glass bottom and bake at 375 degrees for 10 to 12 minutes.

BLUEBERRY MUFFIES

1 pkg. blueberry muffin mix
¾ cup quick rolled oats
¼ cup brown sugar, packed
⅓ cup oil
1 Tbls. milk
1 egg

Drain juice off blueberries; rinse. Drain on paper towel. Combine mix with remaining ingredients; beat well. Drop by spoonsful on ungreased cookie sheet. Make a depression in center of each and press in several blueberries--push dough in several blueberries--push dough up from sides to cover blueberries and pat smooth. Bake at 375 degrees for 8 to 10 minutes until light brown. Yield: 2½ dozen.

DOUBLE CHOCOLATE COOKIES

2 beaten eggs
½ cup milk
½ cup oil
2 cups biscuit mix
2 regular pkgs. instant chocolate
   pudding mix
6-oz. chocolate chips

Combine all ingredients except chips in bowl and beat well. Stir in chips. Drop by spoonsful onto ungreased cookie sheet and bake at 350 degrees for 10 to 12 minutes. Yield: 4 dozen.

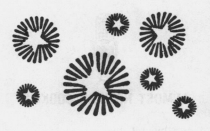

FRUITCAKE BARS

1 can sweetened condensed milk
2 eggs
¼ cup margarine, melted
2 tsp. vanilla flavoring
3 cups biscuit mix
15-oz. jar applesauce
8-oz. pkg. chopped dates
6-oz. jar candied green cherries
6-oz. jar candied red cherries
1 cup chopped nuts
1 cup raisins

Beat sweetened condensed milk, eggs, margarine and flavoring. Add biscuit mix and beat until smooth. Stir in remaining ingredients. Spread into greased jelly roll pan. Bake at 325 degrees for 35 minutes or until done. Cool and sprinkle top with powdered sugar.

PEANUT BUTTER STARS

14-oz. can sweetened condensed milk
2 cups biscuit mix
1 tsp. vanilla flavoring
¾ cup peanut butter
Milk chocolate chips

Mix milk, mix and flavoring until well blended. Stir in peanut butter. Form into 2-inch balls and roll in granulated sugar. Place on greased cookie sheet. Bake for 6 to 8 minutes at 350 degrees. Remove from oven and press 3 or 4 chips onto top of each cookie.

QUICKY MIXY COOKIES

1 cup biscuit mix
⅓ cup cooking oil
1 regular pkg. instant pudding mix
   (coconut flavor suggested)
1 egg

Combine ingredients and mix until dough forms a ball. Shape into balls; place on ungreased baking sheet. Flatten. Bake at 350 degrees for 8 minutes.

ALMOST NOTHING COOKIES

1 cup biscuit mix
1 small box regular or instant
    pudding mix, any flavor
¼ cup milk
¼ cup water

Mix well. Drop by teaspoon on greased cookie sheet and bake at 350 degrees for 10 minutes. Yield: 48 cookies.

PUMPKIN SQUARES

2 cups sugar
1 can pumpkin
½ cup cooking oil
2 eggs
2 cups biscuit mix
1 tsp. cinnamon
1/8 tsp. nutmeg
½ tsp. salt
Nuts and raisins (optional)

Combine sugar, pumpkin, oil and eggs. When well mixed, add remaining ingredients. Spread in greased jelly roll pan. Bake at 350 degrees 20 to 25 minutes (or until tests done). Frost with thin powdered sugar glaze while still warm or serve with whipped topping.

CHOCOLATE BISCUIT PUFFS

10-oz. can refrigerated flaky biscuits
20 bite-sized chocolate peanut butter
    cups

Separate dough into 10 biscuits. Cut each biscuit in two. Remove paper from candy and push one candy into each biscuit half, folding dough completely around candy. (If desired, sprinkle tops with mixture of sugar and cinnamon.) Bake on greased cookie sheet at 375 degrees for 12 minutes or until brown.

CHOCOLATE CHIP-BANANA COOKIES

1 regular-size banana cake mix
½ cup margarine, softened
1 tsp. vanilla flavoring
2 eggs
6-oz. chocolate chips
½ cup nuts

Mix half of dry cake mix into the margarine, flavoring and eggs. When smooth, stir in remaining cake mix, chips and nuts. Drop by teaspoonsful about 2 inches apart on ungreased cookie sheet. Bake at 350 degrees for 10 to 12 minutes. Cool 1 minute before removing from sheet. Yield: 3 to 4 dozen.

BUSY DAY BROWNIES

1 pkg. brownie cake mix
4 squares almond bark, grated

Mix and bake brownies according to directions on box. As soon as brownies come from oven, sprinkle grated almond bark over top. Cool. Cut.

RON'S THROW-TOGETHER SPICE COOKIES

⅓ cup (total) chopped pecans, chopped raisins or dried fruit
1 Tbls. applesauce
2 Tbls. warm water
1/8 tsp. butter flavoring
1/8 tsp. rum flavoring
9-oz. pkg. white cake mix
2 Tbls. shortening
1 Tbls. brown sugar
1 egg, beaten

Combine nuts and/or fruit, applesauce, water and flavorings. Let set 15 minutes. Drain, reserving 2 Tbls. liquid. Combine liquid and drained fruit mixture with remainig ingredients. Beat well. Drop from teaspoon about 3 inches apart on ungreased cookie sheet. Bake 10 to 12 minutes or until light brown. Remove from cookie sheet while warm. Excellent topped with lemon or orange glaze, sprinkled with brown or powdered sugar or frosted with a frosting of your choice.

PECAN PIE BARS

1 regular-size yellow cake mix
½ cup melted margarine
1 egg

Reserve ⅔ cup cake mix for filling. Combine rest with margarine and egg and press into greased 9x13-inch pan. Bake at 350 degrees for 15 to 20 minutes.

Filling

⅔ cup cake mix
1½ cups dark corn syrup
½ cup brown sugar
3 eggs
1 cup chopped pecans

Combine ingredients with exception of pecans and spoon over baked crust. Sprinkle nuts over top. Bake 30 to 35 minutes at 350 degrees.

EASY PEANUT BUTTER DROPS

1 regular-size yellow cake mix
1 cup chunky peanut butter
½ cup margarine
2 eggs
1 tsp. vanilla flavoring

Mix ingredients together well. Drop on greased cookie sheet. Bake at 350 degrees for 10 to 12 minutes.

CREAM CHEESE-PECAN BARS

1 regular-size yellow or white
  cake mix
½ cup softened margarine
1 egg
8-oz. pkg. softened cream cheese
1 lb. box powdered sugar
2 eggs
¾ cup chopped pecans
¼ cup butter brickle toffee bits

Combine cake mix, margarine and egg; mix well. Press into greased 9x13-inch pan for thick, or jelly roll pan for thin, bars. Mix cream cheese, powdered sugar and eggs; spoon over top of cake mix layer. Sprinkle with nuts and bits. Bake at 325 degrees for 40 to 45 minutes.

COCONUT-BANANA BARS

1 regular-size yellow cake mix
2 eggs
½ cup milk
1 cup mashed bananas
Coconut for topping

Beat mix, eggs, milk and bananas together until smooth. Pour into greased 10x15-inch pan. Sprinkle top with coconut. Bake 25 minutes at 350 degrees.

LEMON CAKE MIX BARS

1 regular-size lemon cake mix
1 egg
⅓ cup softened margarine

Combine until crumbly. Reserve 1 cup of crumbly mixture for topping, pat the rest into greased 9x13-inch pan. Bake at 350 degrees for 15 minutes (do not overbake)

Filling

2 eggs
½ tsp. baking powder
¼ tsp. salt
1 cup sugar
¼ cup fresh or frozen lemon juice
½ cup pecans

Beat eggs until foamy; beat in baking powder, salt and sugar until thick and lemon colored. Beat in lemon juice and pour over crust. Combine 1 cup crumbly mixture with pecans. Return to 350 degree oven and bake 15 to 20 minutes or until nicely set and golden on top.

BUTTERSCOTCH SNIPS

1 pkg. butterscotch pie or pudding
  mix
½ cup butter
½ cup brown sugar
1 egg
1 tsp. vanilla flavoring
2 cups flour
½ tsp. soda
½ tsp. cream of tartar
¼ tsp. salt
½ cup nuts
½ cup coconut

Cream together the pudding mix, butter and sugar. Beat in egg and flavoring. Add remaining ingredients in order given and mix well. Form into small balls. Place on greased cookie sheet and flatten with fork in criss-cross pattern. Bake at 350 degrees for 12 minutes or until done. Remove from pan at once.

QUICKY SNACK

Bread slices
Sweetened condensed milk
Coconut
Fresh grated orange peel

Trim crust off bread slices, cut each into 3 strips. Spread on all sides with sweetened condensed milk. Roll in coconut and/or grated orange peel. Place on greased cookie sheet and bake at 350 degrees for 10 to 15 minutes.

UNBAKED CARAMEL COOKIES

2 cups sugar
¾ cup butter or margarine
6-oz. evaporated milk
1 pkg. butterscotch pudding
  (Not Instant)
3½ cups quick rolled oats

Combine sugar, butter and milk in saucepan. Bring to boil, stirring constantly. Add pudding mix: return to boil, stirring. Remove from heat and stir in rolled oats. Cool for about 15 minutes. Drop by spoonsful on wax paper. Yield: 5 dozen.

DOUBLE FROSTING BARS

1 pkg. creamy frosting mix
½ cup flour
¼ tsp. baking powder
1 egg
½ cup chopped nuts

Prepare frosting mix according to directions on package. Mix 1 cup of this prepared frosting with the remaining ingredients. When well blended, spoon mixture into greased 9-inch square baking pan. Bake at 350 degrees for 17 to 20 minutes, or until no fingerprint remains when touched lightly in center. Remove from oven and cool. Frost with reserved frosting. Yield: 2 dozen.

COCONUT CRATERS

1 roll refrigerated sugar cookie dough
3 Tbls. brown sugar
1 Tbls. soft butter
1 Tbls. milk
½ cup flaked coconut
½ crushed chocolate-coated English
   toffee bars

Grease 1¾-inch diameter muffin pans with a little shortening. Cut roll of dough into 9 equal portions. Cut each portion into 4 equal pieces. Put one piece in each muffin cup. Bake at 350 degrees for 8 minutes. Combine remaining ingredients. Remove pans from oven and put a rounded teaspoonful of the coconut mixture in the center of each partially baked cookie. Return to oven and bake about 3 minutes more or until cookies are golden. Cool in pans on rack at least a minute and then carefully remove cookies from pans. Yield: 36.

RAISIN BARS

1 regular-size white cake mix
1 can instant raisin pie filling
3 eggs

Combine and mix well. Pour into greased jelly roll pan. Bake at 350 degrees for 25 minutes. When cool, frost with the following:

Frosting

1 cup brown sugar, packed
1 Tbls. milk
½ cup margarine
1 egg yolk, lightly beaten
1 cup coconut (optional)

Combine all but coconut and boil for 1 to 2 minutes, stirring constantly. Fold in coconut and spread on bars.

WATERGATE DROPS

1 regular-size white cake mix
1 box pistachio instant pudding mix
½ cup oil
3 Tbls. 7-Up
2 eggs, beaten
½ cup chopped nuts
½ cup flaked coconut

Mix in order given. Drop by teaspoonsful on greased cookie sheet 2 inches apart. Bake at 350 degrees for 12 minutes. Remove from cookie sheet.

THREE LAYER NO-BAKE MIX COOKIES

First Layer

½ cup butter
¼ cup sugar
¼ cup cocoa
1 tsp. vanilla flavoring
1 egg, lightly beaten
2 cups graham cracker crumbs
1 cup coconut (optional)
½ cup chopped nuts

Combine first 4 ingredients in top of double boiler. Heat, stirring, until melted and smooth. Stir in egg and cook 5 minutes longer. Remove from heat; add remaining ingredients. Press into 9-inch square pan and cool.

Middle Layer

½ cup butter
3 Tbls. milk
2 tsp. instant vanilla pudding mix
2 cups powdered sugar

Cream butter and beat in rest of ingredients. Spread over first layer.

Top Layer

6-oz. pkg. chocolate chips
1½ Tbls. butter

Melt together in top of double boiler or microwave. Spread on second layer; cut into squares while warm.

QUILT CLUB UNBAKED COOKIES

2 cups sugar
1 5-oz. can evaporated milk
⅔ cup margarine
1 3-oz. pkg. banana instant pudding
1¾ cups rolled oats
1 cup nuts or coconut (optional)

Combine sugar and milk in saucepan and bring to a boil. Add margarine and pudding; stir well. Fold in oats and nuts. Cool. Drop on greased pan or wax paper.

CRUNCHY NUT BARS

2 cups peanut butter
12-oz. pkg. butterscotch chips
12-oz. pkg. chocolate chips
1 cup margarine
½ cup evaporated milk
¼ cup vanilla pudding mix
  (Not Instant)
½ tsp. salt
2 pounds powdered sugar
½ pound salted peanuts

Melt peanut butter and chips together. Spread half in greased jelly roll pan and chill. Combine margarine, milk, pudding mix and salt. Bring to a boil. Remove from heat and stir in powdered sugar. Spread on peanut butter-chip layer. Rewarm reserved chip mixture and stir in peanuts. Spread over filling. Chill.

CHEATER COOKIES

1 all-butter pound cake
¼ cup butter
2 Tbls. sugar
1 tsp. cinnamon

Slice pound cake into ¼-inch thick slices and arrange on greased cookie sheet. Melt the butter and spread over cake slices. Combine sugar and cinnamon; shake over top. Bake at 325 degrees for 25 minutes, until toasted.

FROST AND BAKE COOKIES

1 cup butter or margarine
1 pkg. coconut-pecan frosting mix
2 tsp. vanilla flavoring
1½ cups flour
¼ tsp. salt
½ cup raisins

Soften butter or margarine to room temperature. Cream with dry frosting mix and flavoring. Stir in remaining ingredients. Shape into 1-inch balls and place 1½ inch apart on ungreased cookie sheet. Flatten. Top each with a nut, if desired. Bake at 300 degrees for 15 minutes or until lightly browned.

PROCESSOR UNBAKED COOKIES

¾ cup crunchy peanut butter
3 Tbls. honey
½ cup nonfat dry milk
½ cup raisins
½ tsp. burnt sugar flavoring

Put peanut butter and honey in food processor with metal blade in place. Mix about 5 seconds. Add dry milk powder and process until a ball is formed--about 5 seconds. Quickly mix in raisins--about 1 or 2 seconds. Remove from bowl and shape into small balls. Refrigerate until time to serve. Yield: 2 dozen.

PROCESSOR CHRISTMAS TREATS

½ cup butter
1 cup sugar
1 egg
1 Tbls. cream
1½ tsp. vanilla flavoring
¼ tsp. salt
1 tsp. baking powder
1½ cups flour
Decorations and frostings

Process butter and sugar in processor bowl for 6 seconds. Add egg, cream and flavoring and process 6 more seconds. Add dry ingredients and process 2 more seconds until mixture forms a ball. Wrap in wax paper and chill. Roll out on lightly floured board and cut with cookie cutters. (Add only as much flour as needed to roll out--too much makes the cookies tough.) Place on greased cookie sheet and bake at 375 degrees for 8 minutes, or until done. Decorate as desired.

PROCESSOR ALMOND TREATS

2 cups flour
½ cup almond paste
1½ cups butter or margarine
½ cup powdered sugar
1 egg
1 egg yolk
¾ tsp. almond flavoring
¼ tsp. salt

Cream butter in processor bowl with steel blade. Add almond paste and sugar; process well. Add remaining ingredients. Add a little more flour if needed. Press through cookie press and put on greased cookie sheet. Bake at 350 degrees for 6 to 8 minutes or until just barely brown.

PROCESSOR NUTTY BALLS

1 cup nuts
½ cup butter
1 cup flour
2½ Tbls. sugar
½ tsp. vanilla flavoring
2 tsp. brandy (optional)
Powdered sugar

Toast nuts in small skillet with a tablespoon of butter, stirring. Put into food processor with metal blade in place. Add rest of butter, flour, sugar and flavorings. Process about 30 seconds or until blended. Scrape with spatula and process again until dough makes a ball--about 10 seconds. Turn dough onto lightly floured board and knead once or twice. Roll small pieces of dough into balls. Place on ungreased baking sheet and bake at 325 degrees for 12 minutes. Let cool about 5 minutes on cookie sheet and then remove. While still warm, shake balls in powdered sugar.

ALMOND PASTE

2 cups shelled almonds
1 cup powdered sugar
¼ cup butter
2 egg whites, stiffly beaten

Process almonds in processor bowl with steel blade until ground. Add sugar and butter and process 15 seconds. Beat egg whites separately, and then add to mixture in processor. Blend on and off 4 times. Store in covered jar in refrigerator or freezer. Use in frostings and cookies.

GRIND 'EM UP GRANOLA BARS

½ cup whole figs
½ cup pitted dates
½ cup dried apples
½ cup raisin
½ cup nuts
1 egg
¼ tsp. salt
⅓ cup flour
8-oz. jar marmalade or jam
1 tsp. vanilla flavoring
1 cup rolled oats

Put fruits and nuts in processor bowl with steel blade. Process until chopped. Add egg, salt, flour and jam. Process, then add rolled oats and flavoring. Spread in greased 9x13-inch pan and bake at 300 degrees for about 25 minutes or until done.

ALMOND-CITRUS GOODIES

½ cup almonds
1¾ cups flour
½ cup powdered sugar
3-oz. pkg. cream cheese
⅔ cup butter
2 tsp. lemon juice
¼ tsp. lemon flavoring

Grind almonds in processor bowl using steel blade. Add remaining ingredients. Pat into a 9x12-inch greased baking dish and bake at 350 degrees for 25 minutes. Cool. Top with the following:

Top Layer

3 lemons or 2 oranges
2 cups sugar
Juice from lemons or oranges
4 eggs
3 Tbls. flour
¼ tsp. lemon or orange flavoring
½ tsp. baking powder

Peel lemons or oranges and put peel in processor bowl with steel blade. Add sugar and process until peel is chopped fine. Add juice and then remaining ingredients and blend well. Spread on top of baked crust. Bake at 350 degrees for about 25 minutes. Coconut may be sprinkled over the top before baking, if desired.

PROCESSOR BONBONS

1 pkg. dried fruit
½ cup powdered sugar
2 tsp. corn syrup
½ cup nuts
Powdered sugar for coating

Put steel blade in processor bowl; add dried fruit (apricots are very good in this), sugar and syrup. Process until a ball forms. Add nuts and pulse off and on until just mixed. Remove from bowl and shape into balls. Roll in powdered sugar.

WALNUT OR PECAN PASTE

1½ cup nuts
1½ cups powdered sugar
1 egg white
1 tsp. vanilla flavoring
¼ tsp. salt

Put nuts in processor bowl with steel blade. Process to chop fine--8 to 10 seconds. Add rest of ingredients and process until a stiff paste is made. Scrape down sides of bowl if needed. Put in covered jar and refrigerate. Use as almond paste or marzipan in recipes, or to add flavor to cookies.

HOLIDAY COOKIES

½ cup butter
1 cup sugar
1 egg
1 Tbls. half-and-half
1 tsp. vanilla flavoring
½ tsp. almond flavoring
¼ tsp. salt
1 tsp. baking powder
1½ cups flour

Put steel blade in processor bowl. Add butter and sugar and process 6 seconds. Add egg, half-and-half and flavorings and process 5 seconds. Add rest of ingredients and process 2 or 3 seconds until dough forms a ball. Wrap in wax paper and chill. Roll out on floured board and cut as desired. Frost and decorate according to holiday.

Processor Frosting

1 egg white
¼ tsp. cream of tartar
1 cup powdered sugar
Boiling water
Flavoring as desired

In processor bowl with steel blade in place, beat egg white and cream of tartar until foamy. Add sugar and then drizzle in hot water until consistency desired. Add flavoring if you wish. Hot fruit juice can be substituted for water for more flavor.

CRUNCHY NO-BAKE SQUARES

¾ cup honey
1 cup peanut butter
½ cup instant nonfat dry milk
1 cup chocolate chips
4 cups corn flakes
1 cup coconut

Soften honey and peanut butter in top of double boiler until they blend well. Add remaining ingredients and spread into 9x13-inch greased pan. Refrigerate. Cut into squares.

BUCKAROONS

½ cup butter
2 cups sugar
½ cup milk
3 cups rolled oats
¾ cup peanut butter
6 Tbls. cocoa
1 tsp. vanilla flavoring

Combine butter, sugar and milk in saucepan. Boil for 2 minutes. Stir in rest of ingredients and mix well. Drop by teaspoon on wax paper.

SNOWBALLS

1 cup margarine
1 pound powdered sugar
1 cup coconut
1 cup chocolate chips
2 cups rolled oats
½ cup peanut butter
1 Tbls. vanilla

Combine and mix well. Shape into balls and roll in powdered sugar. Chill.

CHERRY MASH MUNCHIES

2 cups sugar
⅔ cup evaporated milk
12 large marshmallows
½ cup margarine
½ tsp. vanilla flavoring
10-oz. pkg. cherry chips
12-oz. pkg. chocolate chips
¾ cup peanut butter
1 pound salted peanuts

Combine sugar, milk, marshmallows, margarine and flavoring. Melt over low heat, stirring, until mixture boils. Boil for 5 minutes. Remove from heat and stir in cherry chips. Spread in greased 9 x 13-inch pan; chill. Melt chocolate chips and peanut butter together. Crush peanuts and stir in. Spread on top of cherry layer. Chill.

BUTTERSCOTCH BUDDIES

6 Tbls. margarine
1 cup sugar
2 eggs
2½ cups graham cracker crumbs
1 cup coconut
2 cups miniature marshmallows
½ cup nuts
1 cup butterscotch chips
½ cup peanut butter

Mix margarine, sugar and eggs in saucepan. Cook over low heat 5 minutes, stirring. Cool. Mix in crumbs, coconut, marshmallows and nuts. press into 9x13-inch pan. Melt chips and peanut butter together and spread over top. Chill.

SYRUP SUPER-DO COOKIES

¼ cup margarine
50 large marshmallows
6-oz. pkg. butterscotch chips
½ cup chocolate syrup
1 tsp. vanilla flavoring
5 cups crisp rice cereal
¼ to ½ cup chopped walnuts

Combine margarine, marshmallows, chips and syrup in saucepan. Cook over low heat, stirring gently, until melted and smooth. Add rest of ingredients; form into balls. Chill.

ANIMAL CRACKER COOKIES

8-oz. box animal crackers, crushed
1 cup sugar
½ cup soft butter
⅓ cup frozen orange juice
    concentrate, undiluted
⅓ cup chopped nuts

Combine all ingredients. Form into small balls. Roll in coconut if desired. Chill. Yield: 24.

FREEZER SAUCERS

3 Tbls. margarine
6-oz. pkg. chocolate chips
1 egg, beaten
1 tsp. vanilla flavoring
1 cup powdered sugar
¼ cup chopped nuts
2 cups miniature marshmallows
Coconut

Melt margarine and chips together in top of double boiler over hot water. Add egg and beat well. Stir in flavoring, powdered sugar, nuts and marshmallows. Shape into 2 rolls and roll in coconut. Place rolls on cookie sheet and freeze. Wrap in foil or plastic wrap. When ready to use, remove from freezer and slice into neat rounds.

GRAHAM CRACKER MELTAWAYS

½ cup softened butter
1 1-oz. sq. unsweetened chocolate
¼ cup sugar
1 tsp. vanilla flavoring
1 egg, beaten
2 cups graham cracker crumbs
1 cup coconut
½ cup chopped nuts

Mix thoroughly. Press into bottom of 9-inch square pan. Chill while making the following filling:

Filling

¼ cup butter
1 Tbls. milk or cream
2 cups powdered sugar
1 tsp. vanilla flavoring
1½ 1-oz. sq. unsweetened chocolate, melted

Combine ingredients and spread over first layer. Chill partially; cut into squares and refrigerate until completely firm. Yield: 3 to 4 dozen.

ORANGE-RAISIN DROPS

¾ cup sugar
¼ cup frozen orange juice concentrate, undiluted
¼ cup butter or margarine
¼ cup chunky peanut butter
1½ cup rolled oats
½ cup raisins

Combine sugar, orange juice and butter or margarine and heat, stirring, until mixture boils. Remove from heat and add remaining ingredients. Drop by teaspoonsful on waxed paper. Chill until firm. Yield: 30.

CHARMING APRICOT BALLS

4 cups finely chopped dried apricots
4 cups shredded coconut
2 cups finely chopped English walnuts
1 can sweetened condensed milk
¼ tsp. almond flavoring

Combine ingredients in large bowl. Form in 1-inch balls. Roll in powdered sugar if too sticky or if desired. Store in refrigerator.

DARK AND SASSY DROPS

2 cups sugar
2 cups dark corn syrup
2 tsp. vanilla flavoring
¼ tsp. salt
4 cups peanut butter
5 to 8 cups cereal

Combine sugar and syrup. Heat until dissolved, stirring. Add rest of ingredients, stirring in enough cereal to make of drop consistency. (Any dry cereal of your choice--or Chinese noodles--can be used.) Drop on wax paper. Chill. Recipe can be cut in half.

JELLO STRAWBERRIES

2 3-oz. pkgs. strawberry gelatin
1 cup ground pecans
1 cup ground coconut
¾ cup sweetened condensed milk
½ tsp. vanilla flavoring
Red sugar
Slivered almonds
Green food coloring

Combine first 5 ingredients. Chill. Shape into strawberry shapes and roll lightly in red sugar. Color slivered almonds with green coloring and let dry (can dry in microwave oven). Arrange green almonds as stems. Keep refrigerated until time to serve. Pretty to perk up a cookie tray.

FESTIVAL POEM COOKIES

*These cookies are easy and
 fun to make,
Because you don't have to
 cook or bake;
They don't even need a cookie
 cutter.
You start with a beautiful
 stick of butter,
Then mix 2 cups sugar and
 ½ cup milk;
Boil for 1 minute 'til smooth
 as silk.
While it's still hot, add 3 cups
 oatmeal
This ingredient adds a sensational
 appeal.
Now you need ¾ cup peanut
 butter.
It may be hard to stir, but
 please don't give up.
6 tablespoons cocoa and a
 teaspoon vanilla at last,
And look, only a few minutes
 have passed!
Drop them in balls on waxed
 paper to cool.
(If you don't try any, you are a fool.)
Your taste buds should be
 simple to please,
Because of these cookies you
 fixed with ease.*

*(Original poem contributed by a Festival
participant who did not give her name.)*

-65-

UNBAKED SALTINE TREATS

Saltine crackers
1 cup brown sugar
1 cup graham cracker crumbs
½ cup margarine
⅓ cup milk
8-oz. milk chocolate bar

Put layer of whole saltines in greased 9 x 13-inch pan. Combine brown sugar, graham cracker crumbs, margarine and milk in saucepan and cook, stirring often, for 6 minutes. Pour over crackers and top with another layer of whole crackers. Melt the chocolate bar and spread over top. Can sprinkle with chopped nuts.

GRAHAM CRACKER GOODIES

Graham crackers
1 cup margarine, melted
1 cup sugar
1 egg
¼ cup milk
½ cup graham cracker crumbs
½ cup "Bit O' Brickle" pieces
½ cup nuts

Grease a 9 x 13-inch pan and line with layer of crackers. Combine margarine, sugar, egg and milk. Bring to boil, stirring. Cool to room temperature. Stir in graham cracker crumbs, candy pieces and nuts.

Spread over cracker layer. Top with another layer of graham crackers and frost with powdered sugar frosting if desired. (Other candy pieces can be used in this recipe.)

DATE DAINTIES

1 pound dates, chopped
½ cup water
½ cup sugar
1 cup nuts
Round crackers
Whole nuts

Cook dates with water and sugar until thick. Stir in nuts. Spread on crackers and top with whole nut. Or, do not use whole nut but top with second cracker and then frost top with almond flavored powdered sugar icing or melted almond bark.

ETHNIC

ETHNIC

Cookies from faraway places conjure up thoughts of romantic, exotic and glamorous countries. With each ethnic recipe made, visions of places visited or people who have traveled to our shores come to mind. Sharing recipes, in effect, makes us all "kin."

MEXICAN BISCOCHITOS

2½ cups sifted flour
1½ tsp. baking powder
½ tsp. salt
1 cup butter or shortening
¾ cup sugar
1 tsp. anise seeds
1 egg
2 Tbls. brandy (or water)
2 Tbls. sugar
1 tsp. cinnamon

Sift first three ingredients together. Cream butter, sugar and seeds. Beat in egg. Add mixed dry ingredients and liquid. Chill dough. Roll out on floured board to ¼-inch thick. Cut in shapes as desired. Put on ungreased cookie sheet. Combine sugar and cinnamon and sprinkle over cookies. Bake at 350 degrees for 12 minutes or until cream colored. (This is a traditional Mexican Christmas cookie.)

FRENCH MACAROONS

1 cup almond paste
⅔ cup white sugar
¼ cup powdered sugar
2 Tbls. flour
½ tsp. almond flavoring
1 egg white

Chop almond paste into pieces. Mix with remaining ingredients, add enough egg white to make a stiff mixture. Drop on greased, foil-lined cookie sheet. Bake at 325 degrees for 15 minutes or until light brown. Let stand 2 minutes, then cool on rack.

ENGLISH SHREWSBURY TREATS

2½ cups sifted flour
½ tsp. cinnamon
½ tsp. mace
½ cup butter
¼ cup shortening
½ cup sugar
1 egg
¼ cup brandy or white wine

Sift flour and spices together. Cream butter, shortening and sugar: beat in egg. Stir in rest of ingredients. Knead lightly: chill. Roll out and cut in shapes. Bake on ungreased cookie sheet at 350 degrees for 8 minutes or until cream colored.

DUTCH WINDMILLS

1 cup dark brown sugar, packed
3 Tbls. milk
3 cups sifted flour
1½ tsp. cloves
1½ tsp. cinnamon
¼ tsp. ginger
¾ tsp. nutmeg
1/8 tsp. salt
1/8 tsp. baking powder
1¼ cups butter or margarine
¼ cup ground almonds

SOUR CREAM DUTCH KRINGLA

Combine sugar and milk. Beat until smooth. Sift dry ingredients into a large bowl. Cut butter into dry mixture until like cornmeal. Add sugar mixture. Mix well. Refrigerate for 1 hour. Roll dough out on lightly floured board and cut with windmill cookie cutter. Bake on greased cookie sheets for about 12 to 15 minutes at 350 degrees.

For simple sliced cookies--shape dough on lightly floured surface into two rolls about 10 inches long. Wrap each roll in wax paper and refrigerate several hours or overnight. Slice and bake on greased cookie sheets about 15 minutes at 350 degrees. Store in tight container. Yield: 80.

The Hollanders also bake these in great quantities in fancy molds for the eve of St. Nicholas Day, December 5th.

1 cup margarine
2 cups sugar
2 eggs
2 tsp. vanilla flavoring
1½ tsp. salt
1 cup buttermilk
1 cup sour cream
5 tsp. baking powder
2 tsp. soda
5 cups flour

Cream margarine and sugar; beat in eggs, flavoring and salt. Stir in buttermilk and sour cream alternately with soda and flour enough to form a soft dough. Chill at least 1 hour. Roll out to the size of a large pencil and form into a figure 8. Bake on greased baking sheet at 400 degrees for 6 to 8 minutes or until light brown.

SCOTCH CINNAMON-
TOPPED SHORTBREAD

1 pound butter
1 cup brown sugar, packed
¼ cup white sugar
2 egg yolks
1 tsp. vanilla flavoring
4 cups flour
¼ cup sugar
2 tsp. cinnamon

Cream butter and sugars together. Beat in egg yolks, flavoring and flour. Form into balls the size of walnuts. Place on cookie sheet; criss-cross and flatten slightly with fork. Sprinkle tops with mixture of cinnamon and sugar. Bake at 350 degrees for 10 to 12 minutes or until light brown.

FINSBRAD

1 cup butter
½ cup sugar
2 cups flour
1 tsp. vanilla flavoring
A dash of salt
1 egg, beaten
Sugar and nuts for coating

Combine ingredients. Roll pieces of dough to thickness of a finger. Cut into 2-inch lengths and dip in beaten egg; roll in sugar and chopped nuts. Bake on greased cookie sheet at 350 degrees or until light brown.

CZECH COOKIES

Grated rind of ½ lemon
Grated rind of ½ orange
1/8 tsp. cloves
1/8 tsp. anise or fennel
2 oz. nuts, chopped
1 tsp. soda
6 to 7 cups flour
1¼ cups sugar
¾ cup honey
1 egg, lightly beaten
Almonds

Combine grated rinds, spices, nuts, soda and 6 cups flour in a bowl. Heat sugar and honey together to dissolve. Cool and add to dry ingredients. Add enough flour to roll out. Cut into shapes, brush with egg and center with an almond. Bake on greased cookie sheet at 375 degrees until brown--about 8 to 10 minutes.

ITALIAN STRIPS

3 eggs
½ tsp. soda
1/8 tsp. salt
Flour

Beat eggs; blend in soda and salt. Add flour to form a ball. Knead 1 minute, cover and let rest for 1 hour. Roll out; cut into strips 1-inch wide and 6-inches long. Deep fat fry. Frost with powdered sugar icing if desired.

BAVARIAN CHOCOLATE COOKIES

1 regular-size German chocolate cake mix
⅓ cup milk
¼ cup soft margarine
1 egg
1 tsp. mint flavoring
1 cup chocolate chips
1 cup chopped walnuts

Combine mix, milk, margarine and egg. Beat until smooth. Stir in flavoring, chips and nuts. Drop by spoonsful on greased cookie sheet and bake at 350 degrees about 12 to 15 minutes. Cool well. (Can also spread batter into greased 9x13-inch pan and bake for 20 to 30 minutes for bar cookies.)

GERMAN FLAXTWISTS

1 pkg. dry yeast
1 cup lukewarm milk
2 eggs, lightly beaten
1 tsp. salt
Grated rind of 1 lemon
1 cup butter or margarine, melted
4 cups flour
Sugar

Dissolve yeast in lukewarm milk. Beat in eggs, melted butter or margarine, salt and lemon rind. Work in flour to make a soft dough. (Note: there is no sugar in dough.) Cover and let rise until doubled, about 1 hour. Do not punch down dough.

To make cookies: Pinch off a piece of dough; with fingers, shape each into a roll on a pastry board until about 8-inches long and ½-inch thick. Roll in sugar. Fold and twist into shapes as desired--circles, figure eights, pretzels, S-shapes, etc. Place on no-stick cookie sheet and bake at 400 degrees for about 15 minutes. Frost if desired.

GERMAN CHRISTMAS BARS

1¼ cups sugar
1 cup butter
4 eggs, beaten
1¾ cups flour
½ tsp. vanilla flavoring
½ tsp. almond flavoring
Finely chopped black walnuts
Powdered sugar

Cream sugar and butter together until light and fluffy. Add eggs alternately with flour and flavorings. When well mixed, spread as thin as possible on a lightly greased cookie sheet. Dough spreads best if cookie sheet is cold. Sprinkle generously with nuts. Bake at 350 degrees for 12 to 15 minutes or until edges turn brown. Sprinkle with powdered sugar while hot. Cut into bars.

GERMAN WALNUT GOODIES

1¼ cups flour
⅓ cup sugar
½ cup butter
2 Tbls. milk
1 tsp. vanilla flavoring
½ cup chopped walnuts
3 oz. milk chocolate

Mix flour and sugar together. Cut in butter as for pie crust. Add milk and flavoring and mix. Stir in nuts. Chill. Roll thin and cut into rounds. Put on ungreased cookie sheet. Put half a walnut on top if desired. Bake at 350 degrees for 15 minutes or until edges are a light brown. Cool. Melt chocolate over warm water and spread on bottom of each cookie and place on wax paper. Drizzle tops with following glaze:

Glaze

⅓ cup white corn syrup
⅓ cup dark brown sugar, packed

Combine and heat, stirring, to dissolve. Boil 1 minute. Drizzle tops with glaze.

PERSIAN PRETTIES

1 cup butter
1¾ cups brown sugar, packed
1 tsp. vanilla flavoring
2 eggs, beaten
3 cups flour
3 tsp. baking powder
1 tsp. salt
¼ cup milk
⅓ cup nuts, chopped
2 cups coconut
⅓ cup chopped dates
⅓ cup chopped figs
⅓ cup chopped candied cherries
⅓ cup chopped candied pineapple

Cream butter, add sugar and beat until fluffy. Stir in flavoring and eggs. Combine flour, baking powder and salt and add alternately with milk. Stir in remaining ingredients. Drop by teaspoonsful on greased cookie sheet. Bake at 375 degrees for about 10 minutes. Yield: 5 dozen.

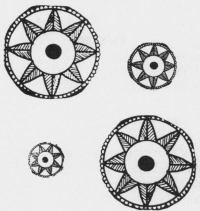

AUSTRIAN WHEELS

½ cup butter or margarine
6 Tbls. sugar
1 tsp. vanilla flavoring
1 cup flour
1 cup finely ground almonds
⅓ cup apricot jam

Cream butter or margarine and add sugar and flavoring. Beat until fluffy. Add flour and almonds. Shape into a roll and wrap in foil. Chill. Cut into thin slices and bake on greased cookie sheet at 350 degrees for 8 to 10 minutes. Spread a thin layer of jam on half the cookies and top with other half. Dip part way into chocolate frosting.

Frosting

1 Tbls. butter
½ cup chocolate chips
1 Tbls. milk
1 Tbls. white corn syrup

Melt ingredients together in top of double boiler. Stir to blend. When melted and smooth, dip cookies into frosting halfway. Put on wax paper to set.

VIENNESE ISCHL TARTLETS

2¾ cups flour
½ tsp. baking powder
1 cup butter or margarine
3-oz. pkg. cream cheese
1 cup sugar
1 egg
½ cup ground almonds
1 Tbls. grated lemon rind
12-oz. raspberry preserves
Powdered sugar

Sift flour and baking powder together. Soften butter or margarine and cream cheese to room temperature and then cream together. Add flour mixture and blend well. Add remaining ingredients with exception of last two. Chill dough several hours. Roll out on lightly floured board. Cut half the cookies in round shapes and the other half in doughnut shapes with a center hole. Bake on ungreased cookie sheet at 350 degrees for about 8 minutes. Cool 1 minute and then remove from cookie sheet. When completely cool, spread round cookies with raspberry preserves. Put a doughnut-shaped cookie on top of each so preserves show through. Sprinkle lightly with powdered sugar. These freeze nicely, but protect with wax paper sheets between each layer. Yield: 3 dozen.

CHINESE FORTUNE COOKIES

3 egg whites
²/₃ cup sugar
Dash salt
½ cup softened butter
½ tsp. vanilla flavoring
½ tsp. almond flavoring
1 cup flour
1 tsp. instant tea powder
2 Tbls. water

Beat egg whites, sugar and salt together. Blend in butter and flavorings and beat until smooth. Stir in flour and instant tea dissolved in water. Chill well. Drop batter on greased cookie sheets, spread with back of spoon to make 3-inch circles. Bake at 375 degrees for 5 minutes or until edges brown. Remove and fold each cookie with fortune paper inside.

CHINESE ALMOND COOKIES

¾ cup butter
1 cup white sugar
1 cup brown sugar, packed
2 eggs
1½ tsp. almond flavoring
3 cups sifted flour
1 tsp. baking powder
¼ tsp. salt
½ cup ground almonds
Whole almonds

Cream butter and sugars until fluffy. Add eggs and flavoring; mix well. Combine flour, baking powder, salt and ground almonds. Gradually add dry ingredients to creamed mixture, mix well. Shape into balls and press on lightly floured wax paper. Press a whole almond into center of each cookie. Transfer to a greased cookie sheet. Bake at 350 degrees for 10 to 12 minutes or until light brown on edges.

MEXICAN PEPPER COOKIES

¾ cup cocoa
1½ cups flour
¼ tsp. salt
1/8 tsp. ground black pepper
1/8 tsp. cayenne pepper
¾ cup butter
1 cup sugar
1 tsp. vanilla flavoring
1 egg

Sift dry ingredients together. Cream butter and sugar together. Beat in flavoring and egg. Stir in dry ingredients. Shape into log and wrap in wax paper. Chill well or freeze. Cut into slices and bake on greased cookie sheets at 375 degrees for about 10 minutes.

DANISH CINNAMON BALLS

1 cup homogenized shortening
1 cup sugar
1 egg
1 tsp. salt
2 cups flour
½ tsp. soda
½ tsp. cream of tartar
1 tsp. cinnamon

Cream shortening and sugar until smooth and creamy. Beat in egg. Sift dry ingredients together and add to creamed mixture. Shape into balls; press flat with fork. Bake at 375 degrees for 8 to 10 minutes.

NORWEGIAN BUTTER COOKIES

½ cup butter
2 hard-cooked egg yolks
¼ cup sugar
1 cup flour
½ tsp. lemon flavoring
Colored sugars

Cream butter and egg yolk which has been pressed through a sieve. Cream in sugar. Add flour and flavoring. Put through cookie press onto ungreased baking sheet. Decorate with colored sugars. Bake at 375 degrees for 10 minutes.

SWEDISH EGG YOLK SPRITZ

1½ cups lightly salted butter
1 cup sugar
3 egg yolks
3 cups flour

Cream butter and sugar; beat in egg yolks. Add flour until dough handles nicely. Put through press onto ungreased cookie sheet; bake at 350 degrees for 8 to 10 minutes.

FRENCH PASTRY SQUARES

Crust

¾ cup margarine
1½ cups flour
3 Tbls. sugar

Combine and press into greased 9x13-inch pan. Bake at 350 degrees for 20 minutes.

Topping

4 eggs, beaten
1 pound brown sugar, packed
2 tsp. soda
1 cup chopped nuts
1 cup coconut
1 tsp. vanilla flavoring

Combine ingredients and mix well. Spread over baked layer. Bake 30 minutes more. Sprinkle with powdered sugar if desired. Cut into bars. Yield: 24.

JEWISH COOKIES

1 cup butter
1 cup flour
¾ cup cornstàrch
⅓ cup powdered sugar
2 tsp. vanilla flavoring

Stir butter to soften, blend in remaining ingredients. Drop by tea-spoonsful on greased cookie sheet. Bake at 350 degrees for 12 minutes. Cool.

HAWAIIAN FRUIT SQUARES

¾ cup flour
1 tsp. baking powder
¼ tsp. salt
¾ cup sugar
2 eggs
½ cup drained crushed pineapple
½ cup chopped dates
½ cup chopped nuts
½ cup flaked coconut

Combine flour, baking powder, salt, sugar and eggs. Blend well on low speed. Fold in remaining ingredients. Spread into 9-inch square greased pan. Bake at 350 degrees for 25 to 30 minutes. Cool slightly, cut into squares and roll each one in powdered sugar. Yield: 36.

RUSSIAN RYE COOKIES

2 eggs
3 Tbls. sugar
2 Tbls. melted butter
2 Tbls. cold sour cream
2 cups fine rye flour
1/8 tsp. soda
1 egg yolk, lightly beaten

Beat 2 eggs and sugar together with wooden spoon. Gradually stir in melted butter and sour cream. Mix flour with soda and add gradually, making a thick dough. Roll thin on floured breadboard. Brush with egg yolk. Make zigzag lines on top and cut into desired shapes. Bake on but-tered cookie sheet at 375 degrees 8 to 10 minutes.

LAPLAND SPRITZ

½ pound butter
⅔ cup sugar
3 egg yolks
1 tsp. almond flavoring
2½ cups flour

Cream butter and sugar together. Beat in egg yolks until light and fluffy. Add flavoring and work in flour a little at a time. Press through a cookie press and shape into small rings or S's. Place on buttered cookie sheet. Bake at 400 degrees 10 to 12 minutes.

SWEDISH GINGERSNAPS

1½ cups flour
1 tsp. soda
1½ tsp. ginger
1 tsp. cinnamon
1/8 tsp. cloves
½ cup butter
¾ cup sugar
1 egg
1½ tsp. dark corn syrup
Whole almonds

Sift flour, soda and spices together. Cream butter, add sugar and beat until fluffy. Stir in egg and corn syrup; beat thoroughly. Blend in dry ingredients in fourths, mixing well after each addition. Chill dough several hours. Roll out on floured board, cut and place on greased cookie sheet. Sprinkle with sugar; put a nut on top. Bake at 375 degrees for 6 to 8 minutes.

FRENCH RAISIN CREAMS

1 cup raisins
Water
1 cup butter
2 cups brown sugar, packed
2 eggs
1 tsp. vanilla flavoring
1 cup raisin juice
1 tsp. soda
3 cups flour
½ tsp. cinnamon
½ tsp. salt
1 cup chopped pecans

Put raisins in small saucepan and cover with water. Simmer about 4 minutes. Remove from fire, strain off juice and reserve. Cream butter and brown sugar. Beat in eggs and flavoring. Combine dry ingredients and stir in alternately with raisin juice. Spoon into greased jelly roll pan. Bake at 350 degrees for about 25 minutes or until done. Frost with a powdered sugar-butter-orange juice icing. Cut into bars.

ENGLISH TEA TIDBITS

½ cup butter
2 Tbls. sugar
1 cup sifted cake flour
Dash of salt
1 tsp. vanilla flavoring
1 cup chopped pecans
Powdered sugar

Cream butter and sugar, add sifted flour and salt, stir in flavoring and nuts. Chill. Form into small balls and bake on lightly greased tin for 15 minutes at 350 degrees. Cool 3 minutes, then roll in powdered sugar. When cool, roll again.

ENGLISH APPLE DESSERT BARS

4 cups peeled and finely diced
  cooking apples
2 cups "crystal" sugar
2 eggs
½ cup cooking oil
2 tsp. vanilla flavoring
2 cups sifted flour
2 tsp. soda
½ tsp. salt
2 tsp. cinnamon
1 cup chopped walnuts

Combine apples and sugar. (The English have a fine sugar called "crystal"--our regular white sugar will work fine.) Let stand ½ hour. Beat eggs slightly. Add oil and flavoring; beat. Combine dry ingredients and stir in alternately with apple-sugar mixture. Stir in nuts. Pour into greased and floured 9x13-inch pan. Bake at 350 degrees for 1 hour. Cool and frost if desired.

PEPPERNUSE

½ cup shortening
½ cup sugar
1 egg, beaten
¼ cup dark corn syrup
¼ cup molasses
½ tsp. soda
2½ Tbls. water
½ tsp. cinnamon
¼ tsp. nutmeg
¼ tsp. white pepper
½ tsp. allspice
½ tsp. anise oil
Dash of cloves
3½ cups flour (or more)

Cream shortening and sugar. Beat in egg, corn syrup and molasses. Dissolve soda in water and add. Mix in spices and enough flour to handle well. Roll into long rolls the thickness of a pencil. Cut into 1-inch pieces. Place on greased cookie sheet and bake at 350 degrees for 10 to 12 minutes. Roll in powdered sugar.

A few of the Drop Cookie entries at KMA's Cookie Contest

SPANISH SEED COOKIES

1 Tbls. whole anise seed
2 Tbls. boiling water
⅔ cup sugar
¾ cup butter or margarine
¼ tsp. soda
1 egg
2 cups flour
Egg for top
⅓ cup sesame seeds
1 Tbls. butter

Combine anise seed and water. Let stand. Cream sugar and butter. Beat in soda and egg. Drain anise seeds and add seeds to mixture. Stir in flour. Wrap dough in wax paper and chill well. Roll dough in small balls and put on ungreased baking sheets. Flatten tops and brush with slightly beaten egg. Top with sesame seeds which have been toasted in a tablespoon of butter. Bake at 400 degrees for 7 or 8 minutes. Yield: 6 dozen.

SCOTTISH DREAM BALLS

¾ cup butter or margarine
½ tsp. vanilla flavoring
½ tsp. almond flavoring
½ cup powdered sugar
¼ cup cornstarch
1¼ cups flour

Combine butter or margarine and flavorings. Blend in powdered sugar and cornstarch. Work in enough flour to roll into balls. Place on ungreased cookie sheet. Flatten with fork dipped In flour to keep from sticking. Bake at 300 degrees for 20 to 25 minutes. Store in tightly covered container. Good keepers.

NORWEGIAN SOUR CREAM KRINGLA

1 cup sugar
1½ cups sour cream
1 tsp. vanilla flavoring
½ tsp. almond flavoring
2½ cups sifted flour
1 tsp. soda
½ tsp. baking powder
¼ tsp. salt

Beat sugar, sour cream and flavorings together until smooth and creamy. Sift dry ingredients together and stir in. Knead a few times on floured board. Take small pieces of dough and form into pretzel shapes. Place on greased baking sheet. Bake at 425 degrees for about 10 minutes. Can glaze with thin powdered sugar icing.

FILLED

FILLED

Filled cookies appear at tea parties, church socials, and other special events which need a spectacular sweet. They can be swirls or sandwiches or kisses. They look fancy but are a pleasure to make and to eat.

BUTTER-ALMOND KISSES

½ cup butter or margarine
½ cup sugar
1 egg
1 tsp. vanilla flavoring
1¼ cups flour
¼ tsp. soda
1/8 tsp. salt
½ cup finely ground almonds
30 milk chocolate kisses

Mix in order given, except for last two items. Form into 1-inch balls; roll in almonds. Put on ungreased cookie sheet; bake at 350 degrees for 10 to 12 minutes. Push kiss in center of each cookie.

CHOCOLATE-MINT TREATS

6-oz. pkg. chocolate chips
2 cups flour
⅔ cup butter or margarine
4 Tbls. white corn syrup
2 tsp. soda
1 egg
½ cup sugar
Round chocolate-covered mints

Melt chips over low heat, stirring. Combine with remaining ingredients with exception of mints. Chill well. Shape into small round balls and bake on ungreased cookie sheet at 350 degrees for 12 to 15 minutes. While still hot, put mints on half the cookies and quickly press a second cookie on top of each. Yield: 48.

CHOCOLATE-PEANUT BUTTER FOLDOVERS

1 cup butter or margarine
2 3-oz. pkgs. cream cheese
2½ cups flour
1 cup chocolate chips
¾ cup creamy peanut butter
½ cup chopped unsalted peanuts
½ cup powdered sugar

Combine butter or margarine, softened cream cheese and flour. Divide into two balls and chill. Prepare filling by melting chips in double boiler. Remove from heat and stir in peanut butter, peanuts and enough powdered sugar to handle well. Roll out cream cheese-dough into 12x12-inch squares; cut each into 25 squares. Place about 2 tsp. filling on each square; spread diagonally to within ½ inch of corners. Bring other 2 corners up and pinch to seal over filling. Place on ungreased cookie sheet and bake at 350 degrees for 15 minutes. Cool on rack.

CHILDREN'S CHOICE

2 ¼ cups flour
½ cup sugar
½ cup brown sugar, packed
½ tsp. soda
½ tsp. salt
½ tsp. cinnamon
½ tsp. nutmeg
1 cup shortening
½ cup peanut butter
¼ cup applesauce
½ tsp. vanilla flavoring
1 egg
1 cup rolled oats
Grape jelly (or jelly of choice)

Lightly spoon flour into measuring cup and level off. In large bowl, combine all ingredients except 1 cup flour, oats and jelly. Mix well. Stir in reserved flour and oats. Shape into 1-inch balls. Place 2-inches apart on ungreased cookie sheets. Flatten with fork dipped in sugar. Press a depression in each cookie with back of spoon and put in a little jelly. Bake at 350 degrees for 12 to 14 minutes or until light brown. Yield: 60.

RAISIN FILLED COOKIES

1 cup shortening
1 cup brown sugar, packed
1 cup white sugar
2 eggs
¼ cup milk
1 tsp. vanilla flavoring
½ tsp. salt
3 cups flour
1 tsp. baking powder
1 tsp. soda
1 additional cup flour

Cream shortening and sugars. Beat in eggs, then milk and flavoring. Combine first flour mixed with salt, baking powder and soda. Blend well. Add enough more flour to make dough easy to handle. Roll into balls and flatten on greased cookie sheet. Put 1 teaspoon raisin filling on half cookies and place second cookie on top, pressing edges with fork to seal. Bake at 350 degrees for 12 to 15 minutes.

Raisin Filling

½ cup sugar
1 beaten egg
Dash of salt
½ cup sour cream
1 cup raisins, chopped or ground

Cook together on low heat, stirring until thick. Cool and use as directed.

COCOA-MINT WAFERS

½ cup butter or margarine
1 cup sugar
1 egg
1 tsp. vanilla flavoring
1¾ cup flour
⅓ cup cocoa
½ tsp. soda
¼ tsp. salt

Cream butter and sugar until light and fluffy. Beat in egg and flavoring. Combine flour, cocoa, soda and salt; stir in. When well mixed, form into a ball; cover and chill for at least 2 hours. Divide dough in half. Roll out each half and cut into 2x8-inch strips. Bake on greased cookie sheets at 375 degrees for 4 to 5 minutes until set but not brown. Cool; then alternate mint filling with strips 5 layers high. Cut into 1-inch pieces.

Creamy Mint Filling

3-oz. pkg. cream cheese
2 Tbls. butter
2 Tbls. milk
1 tsp. vanilla flavoring
1 tsp. mint flavoring
   (or ¼ tsp. peppermint)
1 pound powdered sugar
4 to 5 drops green food coloring

Soften cream cheese to room temperature; blend with butter and milk. Stir in flavorings and enough powdered sugar to make of spreading consistency. Add green food coloring. Spread between strips as directed. These are especially pretty on tea trays.

PINEAPPLE PRETTIES

2 cups flour
½ cup butter or margarine
2 egg yolks, beaten
½ tsp. vanilla flavoring
5 Tbls. cold water
2 egg whites, slightly beaten

Measure flour into bowl. Cut in butter. Combine egg yolks, flavoring and water. Mix into first mixture with a fork. Roll out dough on floured breadboard. Cut into 2- to 3-inch squares. Spoon a teaspoonful pineapple filling on each square. Fold up corners. Brush with egg white. Bake on greased sheet at 400 degrees for about 10 minutes, or until brown.

Pineapple Filling

1½ cups crushed pineapple, drained
½ tsp. pineapple flavoring
⅓ cup pineapple juice
⅓ cup sugar

Combine ingredients and bring to boil, stirring. Reduce heat and simmer until thick, stirring often so filling will not stick. Cool. Use as directed.

PINEAPPLE PINWHEELS

4 cups flour
½ tsp. salt
1 tsp. soda
1 cup shortening
2 cups sugar
3 eggs
½ tsp. lemon flavoring

Sift flour, salt and soda together. Cream shortening and sugar together. Beat in eggs and flavoring. Add dry ingredients to make a stiff dough. Chill. Divide dough and roll out ⅓-inch thick. Spread each with half pineapple-cherry filling and roll up like jelly roll. Chill. Slice ¼-inch thick. Bake on oiled cookie sheet at 375 degrees for 10 to 12 minutes. (Unbaked dough freezes nicely.)

Pineapple-Cherry Filling

2 cups crushed pineapple
1 cup sugar
¼ cup chopped maraschino cherries
½ cup nuts (optional)

Combine undrained pineapple and sugar and cook until clear and thick. Add cherries and nuts.

GALLOPING GOBS

2 cups sugar
½ cup shortening
2 eggs
½ tsp. salt
½ tsp. cinnamon
2 tsp. vanilla flavoring
½ cup cocoa
½ cup boiling water
4½ cups flour
½ tsp. baking powder
2 tsp. soda
1 cup buttermilk or sour cream

Cream sugar and shortening well. Beat in eggs, spices and flavoring. Dissolve cocoa in hot water and stir in. Stir in dry ingredients alternately with buttermilk or sour cream. Drop by teaspoonsful on greased cookie sheet and bake at 350 degrees for 5 to 7 minutes. Fill with following:

Filling

½ cup margarine, softened
Dash salt
1 tsp. vanilla flavoring
2 small or 1 large egg
1 pound powdered sugar

Combine in order given, adding enough powdered sugar to make of spreading consistency. Spread on cookies to make sandwiches.

CHOCOLATE-FROSTED BITTERSWEETS

½ cup butter, softened
½ cup powdered sugar
¼ tsp. salt
1 tsp. vanilla flavoring
1¼ cups flour

Cream butter and sugar until light and fluffy; add salt and flavoring, beating well. Gradually stir in flour, mixing well. Shape dough into small balls and place on ungreased cookie sheet. Press a hole in center of each cookie with thumb. Bake at 350 degrees for 15 minutes or until light brown. While still warm, fill center of each with 1 teaspoon of creamy nut filling. Cool and then frost.

Creamy Nut Filling

3-oz. pkg. cream cheese, softened
1 cup sifted powdered sugar
1 tsp. vanilla flavoring
¾ cup chopped nuts

Combine ingredients and beat until smooth. Use to fill cookies as directed.

Chocolate Frosting

1½ cup chocolate chips
2 Tbls. butter
1 Tbls. water
½ cup powdered sugar

Combine chips, butter and water in small saucepan over low heat. Heat, stirring, until melted. Beat in powdered sugar until of spreading consistency.

MINCEMEAT FOLDOVERS

2 cups flour
¼ cup sugar
1/8 tsp. salt
8-oz. pkg. cream cheese
½ cup margarine
1 cup prepared mincemeat

Combine flour, sugar and salt. Cut in cream cheese and margarine. Knead; divide dough into 4 balls and chill until firm. Roll out each ball and cut with 3-inch round cookie cutter. Place ½ teaspoon mincemeat on half of each and fold other half over. Seal edges with fork. Repeat, keeping dough balls cold until ready to prepare. Bake on greased cookie sheet for 20 minutes at 350 degrees. Cool slightly and drizzle with following:

Glaze

1 cup powdered sugar
2 Tbls. rum (or ½ tsp. rum and
    1½ Tbls. water)
2 tsp. light corn syrup

Combine ingredients and drizzle on warm cookies.

DATE-FILLED OAT COOKIES

1 cup chopped dates
½ cup sugar
¼ cup orange juice
½ cup water
1 cup sifted flour
¼ tsp. salt
¼ tsp. soda
¼ tsp. nutmeg
¾ tsp. cinnamon
½ cup brown sugar, packed
1 tsp. grated lemon peel
½ cup butter or margarine
¼ cup milk
1½ cups rolled oats

Combine dates, sugar, juice and water and cook, stirring, until thick. Set aside to cool. Sift flour, salt, soda and spices together. Add brown sugar and lemon peel. Cut in butter with pastry blender. Add milk and oats. Spread half of dough in greased 8-inch square pan. Spread date filling evenly over top. Roll remaining half of dough between sheets of wax paper into 8-inch square. Fit over filling. Bake at 350 degrees for 25 to 30 minutes. Cool in pan set on rack. Cut. Yield: 2 dozen.

LEMON SNOWDROPS

1 cup butter
½ cup powdered sugar
1 tsp. lemon flavoring
2 cups flour
¼ tsp. salt

Beat first three ingredients together. Add flour and salt. Chill. Shape by level teaspoonsful into balls. Place on ungreased baking sheet; flatten slightly. Bake at 375 degrees for about 8 minutes. Cool. Put two together with lemon butter filling:

Lemon Butter Filling

½ cup sugar
2 Tbls. cornstarch
Dash salt
½ cup water
2 Tbls. butter
2 tsps. grated lemon peel
3 Tbls. lemon juice
¼ tsp. lemon flavoring
3 drops yellow food coloring

Combine first 3 ingredients. Gradually stir in water. Cook, stirring constantly, until mixture thickens and boils. Boil, stirring, for 1 minute. Add remaining ingredients and cool. Spread between cookies.

ANY COOKIE FILLING

7-oz. jar marshmallow creme
2 cups sifted powdered sugar
1 tsp. vanilla flavoring
4 tsp. milk

Cream together with mixer. Beat until light and fluffy. Bake cookies of your choice and use filling between cookies.

PEPPERMINT PATTIES

2½ cups cake flour
2 tsp. baking powder
½ tsp. salt
½ cup shortening
1 cup sugar
1 egg
2 1-oz. sq. unsweetened chocolate
¼ cup evaporated milk

Sift dry ingredients together." Cream shortening, add sugar and beat well. Beat in egg. Melt the chocolate and blend in. Gradually add milk and flour mixture. Blend well. Form into a roll 2-inches in diameter; chill overnight. Cut in thin slices and bake on ungreased cookie sheet. Bake at 400 degrees for 10 to 12 minutes. Put together with peppermint frosting.

Peppermint Frosting

3-oz. pkg. cream cheese
1 tsp. orange juice
½ tsp. grated orange rind
1 cup powdered sugar
¼ tsp. peppermint flavoring

Soften cream cheese to room temperature. Combine with juice, rind and flavoring. Blend in enough powdered sugar to make of spreading consistency.

TAFFY APPLE COOKIES

1 cup plus 2 Tbls. margarine
½ cup powdered sugar
2 egg yolks
1 tsp. vanilla flavoring
3 cups flour
½ tsp. salt
1½ pounds caramels
½ cup water
4 cups finely chopped pecans or
  peanuts

Combine first four ingredients and beat until fluffy. Combine flour and salt; add to first mixture. Roll into little balls about ½-inch in diameter. Place on ungreased cookie sheet and bake at 350 degrees for about 12 minutes. Remove immediately and stick a round toothpick into each. While these are cooling, combine caramels and water in double boiler. Heat over hot water until melted, stir until smooth. Dip each cookie into caramel and let excess drip off. Coat with nuts and wrap in plastic wrap. Great kid treats.

SURPRISE KISS TEA COOKIES

1 cup margarine
½ cup sugar
1 tsp. vanilla flavoring
2⅓ cups flour
¾ cup finely chopped nuts
9-oz. pkg. milk chocolate kisses
Powdered sugar

Soften margarine to room temperature and beat with sugar and flavoring. Stir in flour and nuts. Unwrap kisses; shape 1 tablespoon dough around each kiss to cover. Place on ungreased baking sheets; bake at 375 degrees for 8 to 10 minutes until set but not browned. Remove to rack to cool; roll in powdered sugar. Store in airtight container. When ready to serve, roll in powdered sugar again. Yield: 48.

COCONUT THUMBPRINTS

½ cup butter or margarine
⅓ cup sugar
1 egg yolk
¾ tsp. almond flavoring
1 cup coconut
1¼ cups flour
¼ tsp. salt
Currant jelly

Cream butter and sugar until fluffy. Add egg yolk and flavoring and beat until blended. Stir in coconut. Mix flour and salt together and stir in. Chill. Shape into balls. Place on greased baking sheet. Make a depression in middle of each. Bake at 300 degrees for 20 to 25 minutes. Fill depressions with jelly.

CHOPPED CHERRY KISSES

1 cup butter or margarine
1 cup powdered sugar
2 tsp. maraschino cherry juice
½ tsp. almond flavoring
Few drops red food coloring
2¼ cups flour
½ tsp. salt
½ cup chopped maraschino cherries, drained
48 chocolate kisses, unwrapped

Combine butter or margarine, sugar, juice, flavoring and food coloring and blend well. Lightly spoon flour into cup and level off. Stir flour into first mixture along with salt and cherries. Form dough into 1-inch balls. Bake on greased cookie sheet at 350 degrees for 8 to 10 minutes. Press chocolate kiss into center of each while still warm. Remove to cool. Yield: 48.

PEANUT BUTTER "WICHES"

½ cup shortening
1 cup sugar
1 tsp. vanilla flavoring
1 egg
1¾ cups flour
½ tsp. salt
½ tsp. soda
Peanut butter

Cream shortening, sugar and flavoring together. Beat in egg. Combine dry ingredients and add. Divide dough into 2 portions. Shape into rolls, about 1½ inches in diameter. Wrap in wax paper and chill overnight. Cut slices thin for crisp cookies. Bake on ungreased cookie sheet at 350 degrees for about 10 minutes. Cool. Spread bottom cookie with peanut butter and top with another to make "wiches."

WHIRLIGIGS

1 cup butter or margarine
2 cups sugar
2 eggs
2 tsp. vanilla flavoring
3 cups flour
1 tsp. soda
1 tsp. salt
½ cup peanut butter
2 1-oz. squares chocolate, melted

Cream shortening and sugar. Beat in eggs and flavoring. Sift in flour, soda and salt; blend well. Divide

dough in half. Mix melted chocolate in half and peanut butter in other half. Roll each portion out in rectangles. Place chocolate rectangle on top of peanut butter one. Roll up as for jelly roll. Chill. Slice and bake on greased cookie sheet at 375 degrees for 8 to 10 minutes. Yield: 5 dozen.

CHOCOLATE-CHERRY DROPS

1½ cups flour
½ cup cocoa
¼ tsp. salt
¼ tsp. baking powder
¼ tsp. soda
½ cup margarine, softened
1 cup sugar
1 egg
1½ tsp. vanilla flavoring
10-oz. jar maraschino cherries
6-oz. pkg. chocolate chips
½ cup sweetened condensed milk

Sift dry ingredients together. Cream margarine and sugar. Beat in egg and flavoring. Stir in dry mixture and beat until blended. Shape dough in 1-inch balls and place on ungreased cookie sheet. Push a drained maraschino cherry into the center of each cookie. Heat chocolate chips and sweetened condensed milk together until melted. Spoon about 1 tsp. of frosting over each cherry, spreading to cover. Bake at 350 degrees about 10 minutes. Cool on wire rack. Yield: 48.

BLACK WALNUT FROSTIES

½ cup margarine
1 cup brown sugar, packed
1 egg
1 tsp. vanilla flavoring
2 cups flour
½ tsp. soda
½ tsp. salt

Combine margarine, sugar, egg and flavoring and beat until light and fluffy. Add flour, soda and salt. Shape dough into 1-inch balls. Place on ungreased cookie sheet. Make a depression in center of each cookie and put a teaspoon of filling in each. Bake in a 350 degree oven for 10 to 12 minutes.

Black Walnut Filling

½ cup brown sugar, packed
¼ cup sour cream
1 cup chopped black walnuts

Combine ingredients and fill centers of frosties as directed.

CREAM CHEESE PASTRIES

1 cup butter or margarine
8-oz. pkg. cream cheese
¼ tsp. almond flavoring
¼ tsp. vanilla flavoring
½ cup powdered sugar
2½ cups flour
⅓ tsp. salt
Tart jam or jelly

Soften butter or margarine and cream cheese to room temperature. Blend together and cream until fluffy. Gradually stir in flavorings and sugar. Combine flour and salt and add to creamed mixture. Chill, covered, for several hours. Divide dough in thirds. Roll each portion on well-floured board to 10x12-inch rectangle. Cut with large round cookie cutter. Put a half teaspoon jam or jelly on one side of each cookie. Fold other side over, pinch or press with fork to seal. Bake on ungreased cookie sheet at 375 degrees for 10 to 12 minutes. Yield: 5 dozen.

REFRIGERATOR
ROLLED & CUT

REFRIGERATOR

ROLLED AND CUT

Refrigerator cookies are easy to make and have the delightful quality of staying in the refrigerator for several days or in the freezer for up to 6 months. Because they can keep coming again and again they make excellent, simple busy-day treats.

PINK BEAUTIES

1 cup butter or margarine
1½ cups sugar, divided
3 eggs, separated
2 tsp. grated orange peel
3 cups flour
1/8 tsp. salt
½ tsp. cream of tartar
¼ tsp. peppermint flavoring
Few drops red food coloring

Beat butter and ¾ cup sugar. when light and fluffy, beat in egg yolks and peel. Add flour and salt and mix well. Shape into rolls; wrap with wax paper and chill (or wrap with foil and freeze). When ready to use, slice ¼-inch thick and put on ungreased cookie sheet. Beat egg whites with cream of tartar until foamy. Gradually beat in remaining ¾ cup sugar and flavoring and beat until stiff. Add food coloring to make mixture pink. Drop a teaspoon-ful of the pink meringue on each cookie and bake at 350 degrees for 10 to 12 minutes or until light brown.

LEMON THINS

1 cup butter or margarine
½ cup sugar
1 egg, beaten
1 Tbls. lemon juice
½ tsp. grated lemon peel
¼ tsp. lemon flavoring
2 cups sifted flour
½ tsp. baking powder
Dash of salt

Cream butter and sugar; beat in egg. Add juice, peel and flavoring. Sift dry ingredients together and mix in. Shape into rolls about 1½ inches in diameter. Wrap tightly with wax paper and chill. (For frozen dough, wrap again with foil.) When ready to use, slice very thin and place on ungreased cookie sheet. Bake at 350 degrees for 8 to 10 minutes. Cool on rack.

WHEAT GERM SLICES

1 cup butter or margarine
¾ cup sugar
1 tsp. vanilla flavoring
1 tsp. almond flavoring
¾ cup wheat germ
½ cup ground almonds
1½ cups flour

Beat butter or margarine, sugar and flavorings together. Stir in remaining ingredients. Shape into roll. Wrap in plastic wrap or wax paper and refrigerate until firm. Cut into ¼-inch slices and sprinkle tops with more wheat germ if desired. Bake on ungreased cookie sheet at 350 degrees for 12 to 14 minutes. Let stand a minute or two before removing from pan. (Orange or maple flavoring can be used for variety.)

HEATH HONEYS

1½ cups butter
1½ cups sugar
2 tsp. vanilla flavoring
3 cups flour
¾ tsp. soda
5 Heath candy bars, crushed

Mix all ingredients together. Form into rolls, wrap and chill. Slice ¼-inch thick and put on ungreased cookie sheets. Bake in 350 degree oven for 12 minutes.

SOMETHING EXTRA COOKIES

¾ cup flour
½ tsp. soda
¼ tsp. salt
½ cup brown sugar, packed
½ cup white sugar
½ cup shortening
1 egg
½ tsp. vanilla flavoring
1½ cups rolled oats
¼ cup chopped pecans
Milk chocolate candy bars

Sift flour, soda and salt. Cream together the sugars, shortening, egg and flavoring. When smooth, beat in flour and, lastly, oats and nuts. Shape into roll, wrap and chill. Slice thin and place on greased cookie sheets. Bake at 350 degrees for 8 to 10 minutes. While cookies are still warm, put a square of milk chocolate on each. A half pecan can be put on top if desired.

DATE DO-BE-DOOES

½ cup brown sugar, packed
½ cup white sugar
½ cup butter
1 egg
½ tsp. vanilla flavoring
1 cup chopped dates
¼ cup water
2 cups flour
½ tsp. soda
¼ tsp. salt

Cream sugars, butter, egg and flavoring until fluffy. Cook dates and water together until soft and most of water is gone. Cool. Stir into batter. Add dry ingredients; add a little more flour if needed. Shape into roll, wrap and chill. Slice and place on greased cookie sheet. Bake at 400 degrees for about 8 minutes.

BROWNED BUTTER-PECAN SLICES

1 cup butter
2 cups brown sugar, packed
2 eggs, beaten
1 tsp. maple flavoring
1 cup finely chopped pecans
3 cups flour
1 tsp. soda
¼ tsp. salt
1 tsp. cream of tartar

Put butter in small skillet and stir over medium heat until melted and lightly browned. Stir into brown sugar, add eggs and flavoring. Sift remaining ingredients together and stir in. Form into 2 rolls, wrap and chill for 24 hours. Slice and bake on greased cookie sheet for 10 minutes at 375 degrees.

ORANGE SLICES

1½ cups chopped orange slice candy
½ cup flour
1½ cups brown sugar, packed
½ cup shortening
2 eggs
2 cups sifted flour
1 tsp. soda
½ tsp. salt
½ cup shredded coconut
½ cup rolled oats
½ cup finely chopped walnuts

Dredge candy in ½ cup flour, set aside. Mix ingredients in order given, adding flour-coated candy last. Shape into rolls, wrap and chill or freeze. Cut with serrated knife. Bake on greased cookie sheet about 8 minutes at 375 degrees. Remove immediately from pan.

COFFEE-SPICE COOKIES

1 tsp. instant coffee
1 tsp. hot water
½ cup shortening
¾ cup brown sugar, packed
1 egg
¼ tsp. butter flavoring
½ tsp. vanilla flavoring
1½ cups flour
1 tsp. baking powder
½ tsp. cinnamon
¼ tsp. nutmeg
¼ tsp. salt
⅓ cup chocolate sprinkles

Dissolve instant coffee in hot water. Cream shortening, sugar, egg and flavorings; add coffee. Stir in dry ingredients. Divide into two portions. Shape each into a roll, coat with chocolate sprinkles and wrap in wax paper and chill. Cut into ¼-inch slices and put on ungreased cookie sheets. Bake at 375 degrees for 6 to 8 minutes.

HONEY-APPLE SLICES

¾ cup shortening
½ cup brown sugar, packed
1⅓ cups honey
1 egg
¼ tsp. almond flavoring
1 apple, chopped
2 cups flour
½ tsp. soda
½ tsp. baking powder
¼ tsp. salt

Cream shortening, sugar and honey until smooth and fluffy; beat in egg and flavoring. Fold in peeled, cored and chopped apple. Combine dry ingredients and mix in (add more flour if needed). Divide dough into two portions. Make into rolls and wrap each in plastic wrap or wax paper. Chill or freeze until time to use. Cut into ¼-inch slices and put on greased cookie sheet. Bake at 400 degrees for about 10 minutes or until golden. Watch closely, honey browns more rapidly than sugar. Yield: 5 dozen.

ORANGE-PECAN ICEBOX GOODIES

½ cup butter
½ cup shortening
½ cup brown sugar, packed
½ cup white sugar
1 egg
2 Tbls. orange juice
1 Tbls. orange rind
2¾ cups flour
¼ tsp. soda
½ cup pecans

Cream butter, shortening and sugars well. Add egg, juice and rind. Beat thoroughly. Stir in flour, soda and pecans. Shape into rolls; wrap in wax paper and chill. Slice and bake on greased cookie sheet at 375 degrees for 12 minutes or until done. Makes a nice, tasty cookie. ★☆★

MAPELIES

1 cup butter
1 cup brown sugar, packed
1 tsp. maple flavoring
½ tsp. vanilla flavoring
1½ cups whole wheat flour
1 cup rolled oats
Chopped nuts

Cream butter and sugar; stir in flavoring. Gradually add remaining ingredients. Add more flour if needed to handle well. Make into 2 rolls, coat each roll with chopped nuts; wrap and chill or freeze. Cut into slices and put on greased cookie sheet. Bake at 350 degrees for about 12 minutes. Cool on sheet until firm before removing.

SALTY SNACKS

1 cup butter or margarine
1 cup sugar
1 egg
1 tsp. vanilla flavoring
1¼ cups flour
½ tsp. baking powder
½ tsp. soda
3 cups rolled oats

Cream butter and sugar until fluffy. Beat in egg and flavoring. Sift in dry ingredients and mix well. Stir in oats until dough can be handled. Make into rolls about 1-inch in diameter. Wrap and chill. Cut in slices. Put on greased cookie sheet. Sprinkle top very lightly with salt (yes--salt) and bake at 350 degrees for about 12 minutes. Let cool on sheet. Makes a nice not-so-sweet snack.

CHOCOLATE-MINT SLICES

¼ cup half-and-half
1 Tbls. vinegar
½ cup shortening
1 cup sugar
1 egg
½ tsp. mint flavoring
½ cup cocoa
½ tsp. soda
1/8 tsp. salt
2 cups flour

Combine half-and-half and vinegar, set aside to sour. (Sour cream can be used if preferred.) Cream shortening, sugar and egg until light and fluffy. Beat in flavoring. Combine dry ingredients and add alternately with half-and-half. Add enough flour to handle nicely. Form into long rolls, wrap and chill. Cut into thin slices and place on greased cookie sheet. Bake at 350 degrees about 12 minutes. Cool on racks. Yield: 3 dozen.

Every person should make rolled and cut cookies for the sheer joy of seeing forms emerge from a lump of dough. While these cookies are best done with the assistance of children, it is still fun to make the taste-pleasing treats for yourself or to share. With frostings, sugars and other trims, they become holiday goodies par excellence.

BROWNED-EYED SUSANS

1 cup margarine
1 cup sugar
1 egg
½ tsp. almond flavoring
Yellow food coloring
3¼ cups flour
3 tsp. baking powder
¼ tsp. salt
Chocolate chips

Cream margarine and sugar; beat in egg and flavoring. Add enough coloring to make a pretty yellow. Combine dry ingredients and blend in. Chill if needed to firm dough; roll out on floured board and cut in flower shapes. Put on greased cookie sheets and press several chips into center of each to make the "brown eyes." Bake at 375 degrees for 8 minutes, or until done. Cool on racks.

ALMOND MOONS

¾ cup butter or margarine
1½ cups sugar
¾ tsp. almond flavoring
2 beaten eggs
½ cup ground almonds
2¾ cups sifted flour
1/8 tsp. salt

Cream butter and sugar; add flavoring and eggs and beat well. Stir in almonds, flour and salt. Chill dough. Roll out to ¼-inch thick on floured board. Cut into moon shapes. Bake on ungreased cookie sheet at 350 degrees for about 8 to 10 minutes. Decorate with moon faces if desired.

COOKIE JAMS

1 cup butter or margarine
8-oz. pkg. cream cheese
¼ tsp. almond flavoring
2 cups sifted flour
Jam

Soften butter and cream cheese to room temperature. Beat together. Blend in flavoring and flour. Chill. Roll out to 1/8- to ¼-inch thick. Cut with cookie cutter and place on greased cookie sheet. Spread top of each cookie with jam. Bake at 350 degrees for 10 minutes. Cool on racks.

GINGERBREAD FIGURES

¾ cup sugar
¾ cup butter or margarine
¾ cup molasses
1 egg
3½ cups flour
1½ tsp. baking powder
¾ tsp. soda
½ tsp. salt
2 tsp. cinnamon
1 tsp. ginger
¼ tsp. cloves
¼ tsp. nutmeg
1 tsp. vanilla flavoring

Cream sugar and butter together. Add molasses and egg. Sift 3 cups flour with spices and add, along with flavoring. Stir in enough additional flour to make of rolling consistency. Chill. Roll out on floured board. Cut into desired shapes. Bake on greased cookie sheet at 375 degrees for about 10 minutes. Cool on racks.

SPARKLE CUTOUTS

1 cup butter
1½ cups powdered sugar
1 egg
1 tsp. vanilla flavoring
½ tsp. almond flavoring
2½ cups flour
1 tsp. soda
1 tsp. cream of tartar
Dash of salt
Colored sugars

Cream butter and sugar; beat in egg and flavorings. Mix remaining ingredients with exception of colored sugar. Chill dough. Roll out on floured board. Cut in shapes desired. Put on greased cookie sheets. Sprinkle tops with sugar. Bake at 350 degrees for 10 to 12 minutes. Cool on racks. Yield: 4 dozen.

PLAIN JANES

½ cup butter
½ cup powdered sugar
½ tsp. vanilla flavoring
½ cup finely chopped pecans
1 cup flour
2 Tbls. cornstarch
1/8 tsp. salt
Powdered sugar

Cream butter, sugar and flavoring until fluffy. Beat in remaining ingredients with exception of sugar. Roll out between sheets of wax paper or plastic to ¼-inch thick. Cut into squares, triangles or rectangles. Put on greased cookie sheet and bake at 325 degrees for 12 to 15 minutes. Sprinkle with powdered sugar. Freeze well. Yield: 18.

MOVER WAGON COOKIES

1¾ cups sugar
2 cups butter
4 egg yolks
1 tsp. vanilla flavoring
1 tsp. almond flavoring
8 cups flour
2 tsp. baking powder
1 cup cream or half-and-half

Cream sugar and butter, beat in egg yolks and flavorings. Combine dry ingredients and add alternately with cream or half-and-half. Chill. Roll on floured board 1/8-inch thick. Cut in rectangles and bake over curved pieces of tin to make the cookies look like littled covered wagon tops. Bake at 350 degrees about 10 minutes. Can be frosted. Also good cut in various shapes with cookie cutters.

PLUMP OR SKINNY GINGERBREAD KIDS

½ cup shortening
½ cup light molasses
½ cup sugar
½ Tbls. vinegar
1 beaten egg
3 cups flour
½ tsp. soda
½ tsp. ginger
½ tsp. cinnamon
1/8 tsp. salt

Put shortening, molasses, sugar and vinegar together in a pan and bring to a boil, stirring. Cool. Beat in egg and then add dry ingredients. Chill. Roll out on floured board about 1/8-inch thick for skinny cookies or ¼-inch thick for plump ones. Cut into boy and girl shapes. Bake on greased cookie sheet at 375 degrees for 8 to 12 minutes. Cool 5 minutes, then remove from sheets.

1800 GOODIES

½ cup butter
1 cup sugar
2 tsp. vanilla flavoring
2 eggs
3 cups sifted flour
½ tsp. soda
¼ tsp. mace
¾ cup sour cream
2 Tbls. sugar
1 tsp. cinnamon

Cream first four ingredients. Combine next three ingredients and stir in alternately with cream. Chill. Roll out to ¼-inch thick, cut into shapes; put on greased cookie sheets, sprinkle with last two ingredients mixed together and bake at 350 degrees for 10 minutes. Yield: 5 dozen.

MOLASSES-COCOA CUTUPS

1 cup butter
½ cup sugar
1 cup light molasses
1 egg
1 tsp. vanilla flavoring
3 cups flour
½ tsp. salt
½ cup cocoa

Cream butter, sugar and molasses; beat in egg and flavoring. Add dry ingredients. Chill dough. Roll out on floured board to ¼-inch thick. Cut into squares, circles, triangles, etc. Bake on greased cookie sheet at 350 degrees for 10 minutes. Cool on racks. Frost if desired.

CORNMEAL-RAISIN TREATS

½ cup shortening
¾ cup sugar
1 egg
½ tsp. lemon flavoring
1½ cups flour
½ tsp. baking powder
¼ tsp. salt
½ cup cornmeal
½ tsp. cinnamon
¼ cup milk
½ cup raisins

Cream shortening and sugar; beat in egg and flavoring. Sift dry ingredients together and stir in alternately with milk. Stir in raisins. Roll out to ¼-inch thick on floured board and cut as desired. Put on greased cookie sheet and sprinkle tops with sugar. Bake at 375 degrees for about 12 minutes. Yield: 30.

FANCY FROSTING
(For Any Cookie)

2 egg whites
1½ cups sugar
⅓ cup water
2 tsp. white corn syrup
Dash of salt

Combine all ingredients in top of double boiler. Cook over boiling water, beating constantly, until stiff peaks form. Remove from heat, continue beating until smooth. Frost cookies.

CREAM CHEESE MOONS

1 cup sugar
1 cup margarine or butter
3-oz. pkg. cream cheese
½ tsp. salt
½ tsp. almond flavoring
½ tsp. vanilla flavoring
1 egg yolk
2¼ cups flour
1 egg white
Sugar for topping

Cream sugar, shortening, cream cheese (which has been softened to room temperature), salt and flavorings until light and fluffy. Beat in egg yolk. Add flour. Chill dough. Roll out on lightly floured board and cut into moon shapes. Place on ungreased cookie sheet. Brush with lightly beaten egg white and sprinkle with sugar. Bake at 375 degrees for 7 to 10 minutes. Cool. Decorate with man-in-the-moon faces

---

FROSTED COFFEE COOKIES

2 cups sugar
1 cup butter
1 cup sorghum or molasses
3 eggs
⅔ cup hot coffee
2 tsp. soda
1 tsp. ginger
1 tsp. cinnamon
1/8 tsp. salt
About 8 cups flour

Cream sugar, butter and sorghum. Beat in eggs. Dissolve soda in hot coffee and blend in. Lastly, add spices and enough flour to make so you can roll out dough. Cut as desired and bake at 350 degrees for 8 minutes or until done. Frost.

Old-Fashioned Boiled Frosting

2 cups sugar
¼ cup milk

Combine and boil to soft ball stage. Frost cookies fast, this hardens quickly.

MOM'S HONEY COOKIES

1 cup honey
1 cup sugar
1 cup butter or margarine
1 cup boiling water
2 cups flour
1½ Tbls. soda
1 Tbls. ginger
½ tsp. salt
Additional flour

Dissolve honey, sugar and butter in boiling water; cool slightly. Combine dry ingredients and stir in. Chill this mixture well. Stir in enough flour to roll out. Cut into shapes and bake on a greased cookie sheet at 350 degrees for 10 to 12 minutes. Frost when cool.

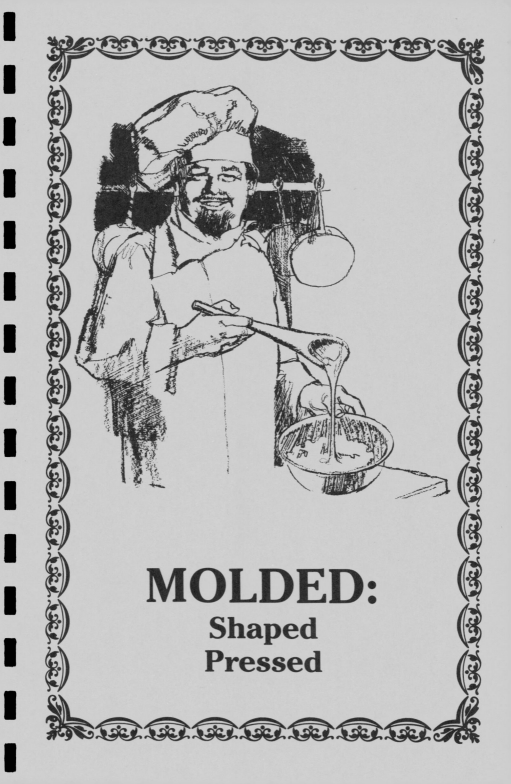

MOLDED:
Shaped
Pressed

MOLDED

Molded cookies can be made in many shapes and sizes. They call forth the creative talents of even the least ambitious cooks. They can be made in circles, twists, crescents, balls and fingers. With the help of a cookie press they turn into stars, ribbons and wreaths. So here are some of the treats which Midwestern cooks enjoy making, shaping and sharing.

COCONUT TOPS

6 Tbls. evaporated milk
3 cups flaked coconut
5/8 cup sugar
1 egg, beaten

Combine ingredients. Shape into small balls and place on greased and floured baking sheet. Bake at 375 degrees for about 12 to 15 minutes or until golden brown. Yield: 2½ dozen.

CHOCOLATE CHIP GOLF BALLS

1 cup brown sugar, packed
1 cup white sugar
1 cup butter (no substitutions)
2 eggs
1 tsp. vanilla flavoring
½ tsp. salt
1 tsp. soda
1 tsp. baking powder
2½ cups flour
1½ cups rolled oats
12-oz. pkg. chocolate chips

Combine ingredients in order given. Roll into golf-ball shapes. Arrange several inches apart on ungreased cookie sheet. Press down lightly with fork. Bake at 400 degrees for 6 to 8 minutes. Do not overbake.

HICKORY NUT BALLS

½ cup butter, melted
¼ cup powdered sugar
1 Tbls. orange flavoring
1 cup sifted flour
1 Tbls. grated orange rind
½ cup chopped hickory nuts
Powdered sugar

Cream butter, sugar and flavoring together. Stir in remaining ingredients. Refrigerate overnight. Make into walnut-sized balls. Put on greased cookie sheet and bake 10 minutes at 350 degrees. Roll in powdered sugar while hot. When cold, roll in sugar again.

SAUCEPAN FUDGE CRACKLES

¼ cup butter or magarine
3 1-oz. sq. unsweetened chocolate
1 cup sugar
2 eggs
1 tsp. vanilla flavoring
½ cup chopped nuts
1 cup flour
1 tsp. baking powder
¼ tsp. salt
3 Tbls. sugar

In heavy 3-quart saucepan, stir butter and chocolate over low heat until melted and smooth; cool. Stir in 1 cup sugar, eggs, flavorings and nuts. Combine flour, baking powder and salt and stir in. Cover and chill until firm enough to shape. Roll into 1½-inch balls and roll balls in remaining 3 Tbls. sugar. Place 2 inches apart on ungreased cookie sheet. Bake at 300 degrees for 20 minutes until crackled on top and slightly firm to the touch. Remove immediately to rack to cool. Yield: 25.

CHEWIES

1 cup shortening (half butter)
1 cup brown sugar, packed
1 tsp. vanilla flavoring
2 cups sifted flour
1 cup chopped walnuts
1 cup grapenut cereal
Egg wash

Cream first three ingredients; stir in next three. Shape into balls. Dip in egg wash made by beating an egg with 1 tablespoon water, then roll in nuts or coconut. Bake on greased cookie sheet at 350 degrees for 15 minutes.

ORANGE JEWEL COOKIES

1½ cups sifted flour
½ tsp. baking powder
½ tsp. soda
½ tsp. salt
⅔ cup shortening
⅔ cup brown sugar, packed
⅔ cup white sugar
1 egg
1 tsp. vanilla flavoring
1½ cups diced orange slice candy
1½ cups quick rolled oats
1 cup coconut

Sift flour, baking powder, soda and salt together. Cream shortening and sugars. Beat in egg and flavoring. Stir in balance of ingredients to make a stiff dough. Shape into balls and place on greased cookie sheet; flatten slightly. Bake at 375 degrees for 10 to 12 minutes. Yield: 4 dozen.

ROSE DELIGHTS

½ cup butter or margarine
1 cup sugar
1 egg
½ cup vegetable oil
Dash of salt
1 tsp. vanilla flavoring
2½ cups flour
1 tsp. soda
1 tsp. cream of tartar

Combine first 6 ingredients. Add remainder and mix well. Shape into 1-inch balls and roll in sugar; put on greased cookie sheets. Using a wire spiral whip, press down on cookies to make rose shapes. Bake at 350 degrees for 10 to 12 minutes.

SHAPED PUMPKIN COOKIES

1 cup butter or margarine
1 cup brown sugar, packed
1 cup white sugar
1 egg
1 tsp. vanilla flavoring
2 cups flour
1 cup rolled oats
1 tsp. soda
1 tsp. cinnamon
½ tsp. salt
1 cup canned pumpkin
1 cup chocolate chips (optional)

Soften butter or margarine to room temperature. Blend in sugars and beat until fluffy. Mix in egg and flavoring. Combine dry ingredients and add alternately with pumpkin, mixing well after each addition. Stir in chips. Drop ¼ cup dough onto lightly greased cookie sheet. Shape into pumpkin shapes. Add a little dough stem to each pumpkin. Bake 20 to 25 minutes at 350 degrees or until cookies are firm and light brown. Remove and cool on racks. Yield: 20.

GROUND RAISIN COOKIES

½ cup margarine
¾ cup sugar
1 egg
½ tsp. lemon flavoring
¾ tsp. cream of tartar
¾ tsp. soda
1½ cups flour
1 cup ground raisins

Mix well in order given. Roll in balls; place on cookie sheets and flatten with fork. Bake 8 to 10 minutes at 375 degrees.

FRUIT NUGGETS

½ cup butter
1 cup sugar
1½ cups flour
½ tsp. baking powder
½ tsp. salt
1 tsp. vanilla flavoring
½ cup candied cherries
½ cup candied pineapple
Walnut halves

Cream butter and sugar. Add dry ingredients and flavoring; blend in candied fruit. Roll into balls and top each with a halved nut. Place on greased cookie sheet and bake at 325 degrees about 30 minutes.

HONEY AND PEANUT BUTTER SAUCERS

¼ cup shortening
½ cup chunky peanut butter
½ cup sugar
½ cup honey
1 egg
1¼ cups sifted flour
½ tsp. baking powder
¾ tsp. soda
¼ tsp. salt

Combine first 5 ingredients; mix well. Blend in dry ingredients. Chill. Roll into balls and place on greased baking sheet. Flatten with fork. Bake about 10 minutes at 375 degrees.

MOCHA NUT BUTTERBALLS

1 cup butter
½ cup sugar
2 tsp. vanilla flavoring
¼ cup cocoa
½ tsp. salt
2 tsp. instant coffee crystals
1¾ cups flour
2 cups chopped nuts
Powdered sugar

Cream butter and sugar together. Add remaining ingredients in order given, except for powdered sugar. Shape into balls and bake on greased cookie sheet at 350 degrees for 10 minutes or until done. While hot roll in powdered sugar.

CRACKER JACKS

1 cup brown sugar, packed
1 cup white sugar
1 cup margarine
2 eggs
2 tsp. vanilla flavoring
1 tsp. soda
1½ cups flour
2 cups rolled oats
2 cups crisp rice cereal
½ cup chopped nuts
1 cup coconut or chocolate chips

Cream sugars, margarine, eggs and flavoring. Stir in soda and flour. Add remaining ingredients and chill. Shape into balls and bake on greased cookie sheet for 12 minutes at 350 degrees.

SHAPED CHEESIES

2 cups shredded sharp cheddar
  cheese
1 cup margarine
2 cups flour
2 cups crisp rice cereal
1/8 tsp. cayenne pepper

Cream cheese and margarine to-gether. Slowly beat in flour; add cereal and pepper. Shape into small balls and put on ungreased cookie sheet. Flatten with a fork and bake at 375 degrees for 10 minutes. *(This is more of a cracker than a cookie, but it came to a KMA Fall Festival and was a nice addition to the cookie table.)*

CHEESY APPLE & OAT COOKIE

¾ cup sugar
½ cup butter
1 egg
1 tsp. vanilla flavoring
¾ cup flour
½ tsp. baking powder
½ tsp. cinnamon
1½ cup rolled oats
1½ cups shredded cheese
1½ cups finely chopped tart apples

Cream first four ingredients together. Sift in flour, baking powder and cinnamon. Stir in oats, cheese and apples. Shape into balls or drop onto ungreased cookie sheet. Bake at 350 degrees for 12 to 15 minutes or until golden. Yield: 4 dozen.

SHAPED SUGAR COOKIES

1 cup margarine
1 cup peanut oil
1 cup white sugar
1 cup powdered sugar
2 eggs
1 tsp. vanilla flavoring
1 tsp. almond flavoring
4½ cups flour
1 tsp. soda
1 tsp. cream of tartar
½ tsp. salt

Mix in order given. Chill overnight. Roll into balls, put on greased cookie sheet and press down with bottom of glass, dipped in sugar. Bake at 375 degrees for 8 to 10 minutes. Pretty sprinkled with sugar.

BISCUIT A LA CUILLER (LADY FINGERS)

¾ cup flour
Pinch salt
4 eggs, separated
½ cups sugar
½ tsp. vanilla flavoring
Powdered sugar

Sift flour and salt together twice. Beat egg yolks with half the sugar and vanilla until light and thick enough to ribbon. Beat egg whites until stiff; gradually beat in remaining sugar and beat 2 minutes or until glossy. Gently fold sifted flour into yolks and then fold the egg whites into this mixture. Spoon batter into pastry bag with ¾-inch tip. Pipe dough about 3½-inches long on a cookie sheet covered with parchment paper or wax paper. Bake in 350 degree oven with door slightly ajar for 15 minutes or until firm on the outside but still soft on the inside. Sprinkle with powdered sugar. Nice for lining bowls for refrigerator desserts.

MINTED MERINGUE TREES

2 egg whites
¼ tsp. cream of tartar
Dash of salt
½ cup sugar
¼ tsp. peppermint flavoring
Few drops green food coloring

Beat egg whites with cream of tartar and salt until foamy and double in volume. Beat in sugar a tablespoon at a time until sugar dissolves and meringue stands in stiff peaks. Fold in flavoring and coloring. Put in pastry bag or cookie press and shape into trees on cookie sheet which has been greased and floured. Sprinkle with sugar or decorative candies. Bake at 225 degrees for 1 hour and 15 minutes or until firm but not brown. Cool 10 minutes on cookie sheet.

PRESSED PEANUT BUTTER PRETTIES

½ cup margarine
½ cup peanut butter
½ cup white sugar
½ cup brown sugar, packed
1 egg
1¼ cups flour
¾ tsp. soda
½ tsp. baking powder
¼ tsp. salt

Soften margarine and blend well with peanut butter. Cream in sugars and egg. Stir in dry ingredients. Chill 1 hour; put in cookie press and shape on greased baking sheet. Bake at 375 degrees for 10 minutes. Yield: 3 dozen.

PRESSED MAPLE RINGS

1 cup butter or margarine
½ cup sugar
1 egg
1 tsp. vanilla flavoring
2½ cups sifted flour
1⅓ cups chopped walnuts
¼ cup maple syrup
Candied cherries for trim

Beat butter or margarine with sugar until light and fluffy. Beat in egg and flavoring. Stir in flour to make a soft dough. Measure out ⅓ cup of batter and mix with nuts and maple syrup and reserve for cookie centers. Put small star tip on pastry bag; fill bag with remaining dough and press into 1½-inch rings on ungreased cookie sheet. Fill center of each ring with a teaspoonful of nut mixture. Bake at 350 degrees for 12 minutes or until golden around the edges. Remove carefully from cookie sheet and decorate with candied cherries.

CREAM CHEESE SPRITZ

1 cup butter
3-oz. pkg. cream cheese
1 cup sugar
1 egg yolk
1 tsp. vanilla flavoring
2½ cups flour, sifted
¼ tsp. salt
¼ tsp. cinnamon (optional)

Soften butter and cream cheese to room temperature and mix together. Cream in sugar. Beat in egg yolk and flavoring. Sift dry ingredients together and add. Put through cookie press onto ungreased cookie sheet. Bake at 350 degrees for 12 minutes or until light brown. Frost if desired with powdered sugar icing.

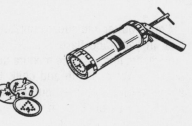

RASPBERRY SPRITZ

½ cup butter
¼ cup shortening
¾ cup sugar
1 tsp. raspberry flavoring
2 Tbls. raspberry jam
1 egg
2¼ cups flour
¼ tsp. baking powder
Dash of salt
Raspberry jam for topping

Cream butter, shortening and sugar until fluffy. Add flavoring, jam and egg; beat well. Sift dry ingredients gradually into first mixture. Chill dough and then put through cookie press onto ungreased cookie sheet. Put a little jam in center of each cookie. Bake at 375 degrees for about 8 minutes. Yield: 6 dozen.

FANCY KANSAS SPRITZ

1 cup butter or margarine
¾ cup sugar
1 egg yolk
1 tsp. almond flavoring
2 cups flour
1 tsp. baking powder
Dash of salt

Cream butter and sugar until fluffy. Beat in yolk, add flavoring. Sift dry ingredients into creamed mixture until blended. Wrap dough and chill. Let dough warm a bit, then put in press and shape as desired on ungreased cookie sheet. Decorate if desired. Bake at 350 degrees for 8 minutes or until golden brown. Cool on racks.

LEMON LETTERS

1 cup butter or margarine
½ cup white sugar
½ cup brown sugar, packed
1 tsp. grated lemon peel
1 Tbls. lemon juice
1 egg
2½ cups sifted flour
¼ tsp. soda

Cream butter and sugars; beat in peel, juice and egg. Combine flour and soda; mix in. Put through press and make letters on ungreased cookie sheet. Bake at 375 degrees for 20 minutes, or until light brown around edges.

PINEAPPLE SPRITZ

1½ cups butter or margarine
1 cup sugar
1 egg
2 Tbls. pineapple juice
4½ cups flour
1 tsp. baking powder

Combine ingredients in order given. Dough will be stiff. Put rosette or other plate on cookie press. Press dough in designs on ungreased baking sheet. Decorate with sugars or candies as desired. Bake at 375 degrees for 8 minutes or until firm but not brown. Cool on racks. Yield: 8½ dozen.

DATE DAINTIES

1 tsp. soda
2 Tbls. hot water
1 cup shortening
1¾ cups sugar
3 eggs, beaten
1 cup coconut
1 cup chopped nuts
3 cups flour
2 cups chopped dates
1 tsp. vanilla flavoring

Stir soda into hot water. Cream shortening and sugar; beat in eggs. Add soda mixture and remaining ingredients. Form into balls and bake on greased cookie sheets at 375 degrees for 12 minutes. Yield: 3 dozen.

BARS

BARS

If a survey is ever made asking people to name their favorite cookie, the chocolate brownie will undoubtedly be near the top of the list. At KMA Festivals and contests the number of bar cookies brought are amazing. They arrive in many flavors, layers, colors and textures. So here are just a few which are easy to make, excellent to eat and perfect for company.

ORANGE BROWNIES

2 1-oz. sq. unsweetened chocolate
½ cup butter
2 eggs
1 cup sugar
1 tsp. vanilla flavoring
¼ tsp. orange flavoring
½ tsp. grated orange peel
½ cup sifted flour
1 cup chopped nuts

Melt chocolate and butter over low heat or in the microwave. Beat eggs; add sugar. Stir in butter and chocolate, flavorings and peel. Beat in flour and nuts. Spoon into greased 8-inch square pan. Bake at 350 degrees for 20 to 25 minutes.

HALLOWEEN BARS

First Layer

2 1-oz. sq. unsweetened chocolate
½ cup butter
1 cup sugar
2 eggs
1 tsp. vanilla flavoring
½ cup flour
½ cup chopped nuts

Melt chocolate and butter together. Stir in sugar, eggs and flavoring. Add flour and nuts. Spoon into greased 8-inch square pan and bake at 320 degrees for 30 minutes. Cool in pan.

Middle Layer

1 cup powdered sugar
2 Tbls. butter
2 tsp. milk
½ tsp. vanilla
Food coloring to make orange

Combine ingredients until smooth adding either orange coloring or red and yellow to make orange pleasing to the eye. Spread over first layer.

Top Layer

¼ cup chocolate chips
2 tsp. butter

Melt together and drizzle over top of middle layer. Cool.

INDIAN BARS

½ cup melted butter
2 2-oz. sq. unsweetened chocolate
  (or 3 Tbls. cocoa)
2 eggs, beaten
1 cup nuts
1 tsp. vanilla flavoring
½ cup flour
1 tsp. baking powder
1 cup sugar

Melt butter and chocolate or cocoa together. Cool slightly and add eggs. Stir in nuts and remaining ingredients. Spread in heavy 8x8-inch pan. Bake 30 minutes at 350 degrees--watch carefully to keep from burning. Cool. Cut into squares. Yield: 16.

❖━━━━━━❖

TOFFEE-MINT BARS

1 cup flour
¼ cup brown sugar, packed
½ cup butter or margarine
30 creme de menthe candies
2 Tbls. water
¼ cup apricot or raspberry preserves
½ cup chopped nuts

Combine flour, sugar and butter with pastry blender until crumbly. Reserve ½ cup of mixture for top. Line an 11x7-inch pan with foil. Pat crumb mixture into pan. Bake at 350 degrees for 15 minutes. Meanwhile, melt candy and water in top of double boiler, stirring, until smooth. Spread preserves over baked crust and spread melted candy over top. Sprinkle with nuts and remaining crumb topping. Bake for 15 minutes more or until golden

❖━━━━━━❖

CHAT 'N CHEW BARS

4 cups rolled oats
1½ cups chopped nuts
1 cup brown sugar, packed
¾ cup melted butter
½ cup honey
1 tsp. vanilla flavoring
1 tsp. salt

Combine ingredients. When well mixed, press firmly into greased jelly roll pan. Bake at 425 degrees for 10 to 12 minutes--mixture will be golden brown and bubbly. Cool. Cut into bars. (Freeze well. Thaw, wrapped, for 2 to 3 hours.)

KIDS SNIPPY DOODLES

2 Tbls. margarine
⅔ cup sugar
1 cup flour
Dash salt
1 tsp. baking powder
1 tsp. cinnamon
½ cup milk
1 egg

Combine everything in a large bowl. Mix well with electric mixer. Pour into greased 9x13-inch pan. Bake at 350 degrees for 15 minutes. Sprinkle with cinnamon and sugar and continue baking for another 10 minutes or until done.

SPICED ZUCCHINI BROWNIE

2 cups sugar
1 cup butter
2 eggs
3 cups flour
2 tsp. cinnamon
¾ tsp. cloves
1 tsp. salt
1½ tsp. soda
2 cups shredded zucchini
2 cups nuts
1 cup raisins

Grease and flour jelly roll pan. Cream sugar and butter. Add eggs. Sift dry ingredients together and stir in. Shred zucchini and press out any moisture; stir in. Add nuts and raisins.

Spread in pan and bake at 350 degrees for 30 minutes. Excellent with cream cheese frosting.

ZUCCHINI ZINGERS

½ cup margarine
½ cup oil
1½ cups sugar
2 eggs
1 tsp. vanilla flavoring
3 Tbls. cocoa
½ tsp. salt
½ tsp. baking powder
½ tsp. soda
2½ cups flour
½ cup sour milk
2 cups grated zucchini
1 cup chocolate chips

Cream shortening, sugar, eggs and flavoring together. Sift dry ingredients and add alternately with milk. Add grated, drained zucchini. Spoon into greased and floured 9x13-inch pan. Sprinkle chocolate chips over top. Bake at 325 degrees for 25 minutes, or until done. (If no sour milk is available, combine ½ cup milk and 2 Tbls. vinegar, set aside for a few minutes to sour. Use as directed.)

SQUASH BARS

2 eggs
1 cup sugar
¾ cups oil
1½ cups flour, divided
1 tsp. baking powder
1 tsp. soda
1 tsp. cinnamon
½ tsp. salt
2 cups seeded, grated squash
   (kuta, zucchini, etc.)
¼ cup chopped nuts
¼ cup raisins

Beat eggs with sugar until light and fluffy. Gradually beat in oil. Combine 1¼ cups flour with other dry ingredients and add to egg mixture alternately with squash. Toss nuts and raisins with remaining flour and stir in. Spoon into greased and floured 9x13-inch pan. Bake at 350 degrees about 30 minutes or until done. Frost or dust with powdered sugar.

BIG RED NEBRASKA BARS

¾ cups flour
¼ tsp. salt
2 Tbls. cocoa
½ tsp. baking powder
½ cup butter
1 tsp. vanilla flavoring
¾ cups sugar
2 eggs
¼ tsp. red food coloring
Marshmallows and nuts for top

Sift dry ingredients together. Cream butter, flavoring, sugar, eggs and coloring together. Add dry ingredients. Bake in greased 9x9-inch pan at 350 degrees for about 25 minutes. Sprinkle marshmallows and nuts over bars. Return to oven for 1 minute, just long enough to melt the marshmallows. Can top with chocolate frosting if desired.

MERINGUE BARS

½ cup butter
1 cup sugar
1 egg
1 egg yolk
1½ cups flour
1½ tsp. baking powder
1 tsp. vanilla flavoring
1 egg white
1 cup brown sugar, packed
½ cup chopped nuts
½ tsp. vanilla flavoring

Cream butter and first cup sugar; add whole egg and yolk. Sift flour and baking powder and add. Stir in first flavoring. Pat dough into greased 9x13-inch pan. Make meringue by beating egg white until stiff, gradually beat in brown sugar. When stiff peaks form, fold in nuts and remaining flavoring. Spread the meringue over top of dough. Bake at 375 degrees for 15 minutes.

CANDIED CARAMEL BARS

14-oz. pkg. caramel candy
1/3 cup milk
2 cups flour
2 cups rolled oats
1½ cups brown sugar, packed
1 tsp. soda
½ tsp. salt
1 egg
1 cup butter or margarine
Chocolate chips and nuts

Heat candy and milk over low heat, stirring, until melted and blended. Combine flour, oats, sugar, soda, salt and egg. Stir in butter with fork until crumbly. Press half of mixture into 9x13-inch greased pan. Bake 10 minutes at 350 degrees. Sprinkle with chips and nuts and drizzle with caramel mixture. Sprinkle rest of crumb mixture over top. Bake 20 to 30 minutes. Cool 30 minutes. Loosen edges from pan; cool and cut into bars. Yield: 54.

MALTED MILK BARS

2/3 cup sifted flour
3/4 cup chocolate malted milk powder
½ tsp. baking powder
1/3 cup butter, melted
3/4 cup brown sugar, packed
2 eggs
½ tsp. vanilla flavoring
½ cup nuts

Sift dry ingredients together. Combine melted butter and brown sugar and beat well. Beat in eggs. Stir in dry mixture, flavoring and nuts. Spread in greased 9-inch square pan. Bake at 350 degrees for 25 to 30 minutes.

Frosting

2½ Tbls. malted milk powder
¼ cup margarine
¼ cup evaporated milk or
   half-and-half
¼ cup brown sugar, packed
Powdered sugar

Heat everything together with exception of powdered sugar. Stir in enough powdered sugar to spread.

APRICOT PRESERVE BARS

½ cup margarine
1½ cups rolled oats
1½ cup flour
1 cup brown sugar, packed
1 tsp. baking powder
1 tsp. vanilla flavoring
16-oz. jar apricot preserves

Combine all ingredients with exception of preserves. Pat half this mixture into a greased 9x13-inch pan. Spread on preserves and top with other half crumb mixture. Bake at 350 degrees for 30 minutes or until done.

DOUBLE APPLE BARS

1½ cups flour
½ tsp. baking powder
½ tsp. soda
¼ tsp. cloves
1 tsp. cinnamon
¼ cup butter or margarine
½ cup brown sugar, packed
1 large egg
1 cup applesauce
2 cups peeled and diced apples
½ cup chopped pecans
2 Tbls. brown sugar, packed
1 cup chopped pecans

Combine flour, baking powder, soda and spices. Cream butter and ½ cup sugar together until fluffy. Add egg, then flour mixture. Fold in applesauce and apples and ½ cup nuts. Spread evenly in greased and floured 9x13-inch pan. Mix remaining 2 Tbls. brown sugar and 1 cup nuts and sprinkle over top. Bake for 35 minutes at 375 degrees.

PICNIC BARS

1 cup rolled oats
½ cup margarine
1½ cups boiling water
2 eggs
1 cup brown sugar, packed
1 cup white sugar
1½ cups flour
1 tsp. soda
1 tsp. cinnamon
⅓ tsp. salt

Combine rolled oats, margarine and boiling water. Set aside to cool. Beat in eggs and sugars. Combine remaining ingredients and stir in. Spoon into greased jelly roll pan and bake at 350 degrees for 30 minutes or until done. Do not overbake. Frost with caramel frosting if desired.

Caramel Frosting

1½ cups brown sugar, packed
¾ cup evaporated milk
¼ cup margarine
1 tsp. vanilla flavoring
½ tsp. burnt sugar flavoring
Powdered sugar

Combine first 3 ingredients in saucepan and cook, stirring, until sugar dissolves and margarine is melted. Remove from heat and stir in flavorings and enough powdered sugar to make spreadable.

CRUNCHY APPLE BARS

½ cup shortening
1 cup sugar
1 cup applesauce
2 cups flour
1 tsp. soda
1 tsp. nutmeg
1½ tsp. cinnamon
¼ tsp. cloves
¼ tsp. salt
1 tsp. vanilla flavoring
1 cup raisins
¼ cup nuts
¾ cup crushed cornflakes
¼ cup sugar
2 Tbls. melted butter
¼ cup chopped nuts

Cream shortening and 1 cup sugar. Beat in applesauce. Sift dry ingredients together and mix in; add flavoring. Stir in raisins and nuts. Spread on greased jelly roll pan. Combine cereal, ¼ cup sugar, melted butter and nuts. Sprinkle over top of batter. Bake at 350 degrees for 30 minutes.

TANGY APPLE TREATS

½ cup butter
¾ cup sugar
2 eggs
1 cup sifted flour
1 tsp. baking powder
½ tsp. soda
½ tsp. salt
1 Tbls. cocoa
1 tsp. cinnamon
1 cup rolled oats
1½ cups peeled, diced apples
½ cup chopped walnuts

Cream butter and sugar, beat in eggs, one at a time, beating well after each. Sift dry ingredients together (¼ tsp. each of nutmeg and cloves can be added if you like more spices). Add to first mixture. Stir in rest of ingredients. Spread in greased 9x13-inch pan. Bake at 375 degrees for 25 minutes. When slightly cool, cut into bars and sprinkle with powdered sugar or frost with the following.

Tangy Icing

2 Tbls. orange or lemon juice
¾ cup powdered sugar

Combine ingredients and beat until creamy. Spread over bars.

RHUBARB BARS

1 cup flour
⅓ cup powdered sugar
½ cup butter or margarine
2 eggs
1 cup sugar
¼ cup flour
½ tsp. salt
2 cups finely chopped rhubarb
1½ tsp. vanilla flavoring

Combine 1 cup flour and powdered sugar. Cut in shortening until crumbly. Press into ungreased 9x13-inch pan. Bake at 350 degrees for 15 minutes or until light brown around edges. Beat eggs and stir in 1 cup sugar, remaining ¼ cup flour and salt. Add rhubarb and flavoring. Put over bottom crust. Bake for 30 to 35 minutes.

GREEN TOMATO MINCEMEAT BARS

2 cups flour
1 cup sugar
½ tsp. soda
½ tsp. salt
½ cup oil
¼ cup evaporated milk
4 cups mincemeat, drained

Mix dry ingredients. Add rest and mix well. Spread on greased jelly roll pan and bake 30 minutes in a 375 degree oven, or until done. (Note: No eggs in this recipe.) Many a frugal Midwestern cook cans green tomato mincemeat at the end of the gardening season.

MINCEMEAT SQUARES

1 cup sifted flour
1 tsp. baking powder
¼ tsp. salt
6 Tbls. sugar
¼ cup melted shortening
1 egg
¼ tsp. orange flavoring
1½ tsp. grated orange rind
6 Tbls. prepared mincemeat

Sift first three items together. Cream sugar and shortening; add egg and beat until smooth. Stir in flavoring. Gradually beat in dry ingredients. When well blended, put half the dough in 8x8-inch greased pan. Combine mincemeat and orange rind and spread over first layer; top with remaining dough. Bake at 375 degrees for 25 to 30 minutes. Can glaze if desired.

MARSHMALLOW CREME-BANANA BARS

1½ cups sugar
⅔ cup butter
2 eggs
½ tsp. vanilla flavoring
1 cup mashed bananas
1 tsp. soda
¼ tsp. salt
2 cups flour
¼ cup milk
½ cup nuts
7-oz. jar marshmallow creme

Cream sugar and butter together. Beat in eggs, flavoring and bananas. Combine dry ingredients and add alternately with milk. Mix in nuts. Put in greased jelly roll pan and bake at 350 degrees for 20 to 25 minutes. While warm, spread with marshmallow creme.

BANANA BANGERS

½ cup butter or margarine
1 cup sugar
1 egg
1 tsp. soda
1 Tbls. water
1 tsp. vanilla flavoring
¼ tsp. banana flavoring
1⅓ cup mashed bananas
1½ cups flour
1 tsp. baking powder
Dash of salt

Cream butter and sugar. Beat in egg. Dissolve soda in water and add to first mixture along with flavorings. Add bananas. Sift dry ingredients together and beat in. Spread in greased jelly roll pan and bake at 350 degrees for 25 to 30 minutes.

ALMOND BARS

Crust

3 cups flour
1 tsp. salt
1/8 tsp. baking powder
1 cup shortening
1 egg
1 tsp. vinegar
5 Tbls. water

Combine dry ingredients; cut in shortening. Beat remaining ingredients together and mix into first mixture. Roll out half and put in 9x13-inch pan. Fill with following filling:

Filling

1½ cups sugar
2 eggs
6 Tbls. flour
½ cup milk
3 tsp. almond flavoring

Combine and bring to boil. (Can do this in microwave.) Pour into crust-lined pan and top with remaining crust. Bake at 375 degrees for 30 to 35 minutes or until brown.

CHERRY-WALNUT BARS

Crust

2 ¼ cups flour
½ cup sugar
1 cup butter

Combine and press into 9x13-inch pan. Bake for 15 minutes at 350 degrees.

Filling

2 eggs
1 egg yolk
1 ½ cups brown sugar, packed
½ tsp. baking powder
½ cup chopped walnuts
½ tsp. salt
½ cup chopped maraschino cherries

Blend together in order given. Spoon over top of baked crust. Return to oven for 20 to 25 minutes. When cool, ice.

Icing

1 unbeaten egg white
2 Tbls. melted butter
2 Tbls. cherry juice
2 cups powdered sugar

Combine and mix with electric beater until smooth and creamy. Ice bars.

CHEESECAKE BARS

1 cup flour
½ cup brown sugar, packed
½ cup chopped walnuts
⅓ cup butter or margarine
8-oz. pkg. cream cheese
¼ cup white sugar
1 large egg
1 Tbls. lemon juice
2 Tbls. milk
1 tsp. vanilla flavoring

With a fork, stir first four ingredients together until crumbly. Reserve 1 cup of this mixture for topping. Press remainder into greased 8-inch square pan and bake at 350 degrees for 12 to 15 minutes. Beat together the remaining ingredients and pour into baked crust; sprinkle with reserved crumb mixture. Bake about 25 minutes. Cool and cut. Store in refrigerator.

SIMPLE BROWNIES

½ cup margarine
1 cup sugar
Dash salt
2 eggs
½ tsp. vanilla flavoring
¾ cup flour
¼ cup cocoa

Beat together in order given. Put in greased 8x8-inch pan. Bake at 350 degrees about 20 minutes. Do not overbake.

SALTED PEANUT CHEWS

1½ cups flour
¼ tsp. baking powder
¼ tsp. soda
⅔ cup brown sugar
½ tsp. salt
1 tsp. vanilla flavoring
½ cup margarine
2 egg yolks
3 cups marshmallows

Combine all ingredients except marshmallows. Mix until crumbly. Press into ungreased 9x13-inch pan. Bake at 350 degrees for 12 to 15 minutes. Immediately sprinkle marshmallows on top. Return to oven for 1 or 2 minutes until puffy. Cool and prepare the topping.

Topping

⅔ cup corn syrup
¼ cup margarine
2 tsp. vanilla
12-oz. pkg. peanut butter chips
2 cups crisp rice cereal
2 cups cocktail peanuts

In saucepan, heat corn syrup, margarine, flavoring and peanut butter chips just until melted and smooth. Stir constantly. Remove from heat, stir in cereal and nuts. Immediately, spoon warm topping over marshmallow layer; spread to cover. Chill.

LEMON-COCONUT SQUARES

Crust

1½ cups sifted flour
½ cup brown sugar, packed
½ cup butter or margarine

Mix until crumbly. Pat into greased 9x13-inch pan. Bake at 275 degrees for 10 minutes. Spread following filling over top:

Filling

2 eggs, beaten
1 cup brown sugar, packed
1½ cups flaked coconut
1 cup chopped nuts
2 Tbls. flour
½ tsp. baking powder
¼ tsp. salt
½ tsp. vanilla flavoring

Combine ingredients in order given, mixing well. Spoon over crust. Bake at 350 degrees for 20 minutes and frost with the following:

Frosting

1 cup powdered sugar
1 Tbls. melted butter
Juice of 1 lemon

Combine, using enough powdered sugar to make spreadable. Frost bars while still warm.

SAUCEPAN PINEAPPLE BARS

½ cup margarine
⅓ cup white sugar
⅓ cup brown sugar, packed
1 Tbls. lemon juice
1 cup sifted flour
1¼ tsp. baking powder
1 egg
½ cup chopped nuts
½ cup crushed, drained pineapple

Melt margarine in saucepan. Remove from heat. Add sugars and lemon juice, blend. Stir in flour and baking powder. Beat in egg. Fold in nuts and pineapple. Pour into greased 9x9-inch pan. Bake at 350 degrees about 30 minutes. Do not overbake. Cool in pan.

WHITE FROSTED DELIGHTS

1½ cups sifted cake flour
½ tsp. salt
1 tsp. baking powder
½ cup shortening
1 cup sugar
2 eggs, beaten
½ tsp. vanilla flavoring
1 cup brown sugar, packed
1 egg white, stiffly beaten

Sift flour, salt and baking powder together. Cream shortening and sugar until fluffy. Add eggs, flavoring and sifted dry ingredients and mix well. Spread in greased jelly roll pan. Beat brown sugar and egg white together and spread over batter. Sprinkle with nuts if desired. Bake at 325 degrees for 30 minutes.

SPONGE BARS

4 eggs, beaten
2 cups sugar
2 cups flour
½ tsp. salt
1 tsp. vanilla flavoring
2 tsp. baking powder
1 cup water

Beat eggs until thick. Add sugar and beat 6 minutes. Add rest of ingredients and beat until well mixed. Bake on greased and floured jelly roll pan at 350 degrees for 20 minutes. Frost.

Frosting

1 egg
½ cup butter or margarine
1 tsp. vanilla flavoring
2 cups powdered sugar
Crushed salted peanuts for topping

Beat egg, butter and flavoring with powdered sugar. Frost bars and top with peanuts.

PRESERVE CHEWIES

¾ cup butter or margarine
¾ cup sugar, divided
2 eggs, separated
1½ cups sifted flour
1 cup chopped nuts
1 cup fruit preserves
½ cup coconut

Cream butter and ¼ cup sugar; beat in egg yolks. Stir in flour. Spread in greased 9x13-inch pan. Bake at 350 degrees for 15 minutes. Beat egg whites until light peaks form, gradually beat in ½ cup sugar until stiff. Fold in nuts. Spread preserves over first layer, top with egg white mixture. Bake at 350 degrees for 25 minutes. Cut into small squares.

ICED GINGER BARS

2 cups flour
1 cup sugar
1 tsp. soda
1 tsp. cinnamon
1 tsp. ginger
1 tsp. cloves
1 cup hot coffee
1 cup margarine
½ cup molasses
2 eggs

Combine ingredients in large bowl and beat well. Bake in greased jelly roll pan at 350 degrees for 30 minutes. Frost:

Frosting

⅓ cup browned butter
2 Tbls. hot water
Powdered sugar

Heat butter in skillet over low heat, stirring, until brown. Stir in hot water and powdered sugar to spread.

MAPLE-WALNUT BARS

¼ cup butter or margarine
½ cup sugar
1 egg
½ tsp. maple flavoring
1 cup flour
½ tsp. baking powder
½ tsp. soda
½ cup milk
½ cup chopped walnuts

Cream butter and sugar, beat in egg and flavoring. Sift dry ingredients and mix in alternately with milk. Spread in greased 11x7-inch pan. Bake at 350 degrees for 25 minutes. Drizzle with maple glaze.

Maple Glaze

⅔ cup sifted powdered sugar
⅓ cup milk
3 Tbls. butter
½ tsp. maple flavoring

Combine, bring to boil, stirring. Use on bars as directed.

ALMOND DELIGHTS

1 cup butter
¾ cups sugar
1 egg, separated
½ cup almond paste
1 tsp. almond flavoring
2 cups flour
¼ cup chopped almonds

Cream butter and sugar, add egg yolk, almond paste and flavoring; mix well. Stir in flour. Press in greased 8-inch square pan. Beat egg white with fork until frothy and spread over top. Top with nuts. Bake at 350 degrees for 30 minutes. Cool and cut. Wrap in plastic wrap to store.

DATE-FILLED BARS

1 cup chopped dates
½ cup sugar
½ cup orange juice
½ cup water
1 cup sifted flour
¼ tsp. salt
¼ tsp. soda
¼ tsp. nutmeg
¾ tsp. cinnamon
½ cup brown sugar, packed
1 tsp. grated lemon peel
½ cup butter or margarine
¼ cup milk
1½ cups rolled oats

Combine dates, ½ cup sugar, juice and water. Cook, stirring, until thick.

Cool. Sift flour, salt, soda and spices together. Add brown sugar and lemon peel. Cut in butter. Stir in milk and oats. Press half of dough into a greased 8-inch square pan. Spread date filling evenly over top. Roll remaining half of dough between sheets of waxed paper into an 8-inch square. Fit over date layer. Bake at 350 degrees for 25 to 30 minutes

APRICOT-DATE BARS

1½ cups dried apricots
1 cup chopped dates
1 cup water
½ cup sugar
1 tsp. grated lemon peel
¼ tsp. lemon flavoring
½ cup nuts
1 cup brown sugar, packed
¾ cup butter
2 cups flour
2 cups rolled oats
1 tsp. soda
1 tsp. vanilla flavoring

Combine chopped apricots, dates and water. Cook until tender. Stir in ½ cup sugar and continue cooking until mixture is thick. Add lemon peel, lemon flavoring and nuts. Cool. Cream brown sugar and butter; mix in rest of ingredients. Press half of mixture into 9x13-inch greased pan. Spread with apricot-date mixture. Top with remaining crumbs. Bake at 375 degrees for 35 minutes.

SOUR CREAM-BANANA BARS

1½ cups margarine
1½ cups sugar
2 eggs, beaten
2 cups mashed bananas
1 tsp. vanilla flavoring
¾ cup sour cream
2 cups flour
¼ tsp. salt
1 tsp. soda

Cream margarine and sugar; mix in eggs. Add bananas, flavoring and sour cream. Sift dry ingredients and stir in. Put in greased jelly roll pan at 350 degrees for 25 to 30 minutes. Frost with following:

Sour Cream Frosting

¼ cup margarine
¼ cup sour cream
½ tsp. vanilla flavoring
1 Tbls. water
Powdered sugar

Combine ingredients with enough powdered sugar to spread.

FUN SYRUP BROWNIES

½ cup margarine
1 cup sugar
4 eggs
1 tsp. vanilla flavoring
1¼ cups flour
¼ tsp. baking powder
16-oz. can chocolate syrup

Cream margarine and sugar, beat in eggs one at a time. Blend in remaining ingredients in order given. Beat well. Bake in greased jelly roll pan at 350 degrees for about 30 minutes. Frost with chocolate or white icing if desired.

SCOTTY BARS

6 Tbls. butter or margarine
½ cup brown sugar, packed
1 cup sifted flour
2 eggs
1 cup brown sugar, packed
1½ tsp. vanilla flavoring
¼ cup flour
1 tsp. baking powder
½ tsp. salt
½ cup chopped walnuts
6-oz. pkg. butterscotch chips

Cream butter or margarine and ½ cup brown sugar until fluffy. Blend in 1 cup flour. Pat into ungreased 11x7-inch pan. Bake at 350 degrees for 10 minutes. Beat eggs until thick, beat in 1 cup brown sugar and vanilla. Combine remaining flour, baking powder and salt; add to egg mixture. Stir in nuts. Spread over baked crust. Sprinkle with chips. Bake 30 minutes more. Yield: 15 bars.

CINNAMON DRIZZLED BARS

¼ cup sugar
1 cup water
1 Tbls. cornstarch
2 cups raisins
1 tsp. lemon juice
½ cup margarine
1 cup brown sugar, packed
1 tsp. vanilla
1½ cups flour
½ tsp. soda
¼ tsp. salt
1½ cups rolled oats
1 Tbls. water

Combine first five ingredients. Cook, stirring, over medium heat until thick and clear. Cool. Cream margarine, brown sugar and flavoring. Sift dry ingredients together and stir in. Add oats and water. Pat half this mixture into 9x13-inch greased pan. Spread with raisin mixture. Add another tablespoon water to remaining crumb mixture and spoon over top of second layer. Pat smooth. Bake at 350 degrees for 30 to 35 minutes. While warm, drizzle with cinnamon icing. Good with ice cream on top.

Cinnamon Icing

1 cup powdered sugar
¼ tsp. cinnamon
½ tsp. vanilla
Milk

Combine with enough milk to make of drizzling consistency.

PEACHY OATMEAL BARS

¾ cup margarine
1¼ cups rolled oats
1¼ cups flour
½ cup sugar
1½ tsp. baking powder
2 tsp. cinnamon
1 cup peach preserves
¾ cup flaked coconut

Melt margarine in 9x13-inch pan. Cool slightly, stir in dry ingredients until blended. Mixture will be crumbly. Reserve ½ cup crumb mixture and press rest firmly into bottom of pan. Spread preserves to within ½ inch of edges. Sprinkle with reserved crumbs and top with coconut. Bake 25 minutes at 350 degrees or until edges are lightly browned. Yield: 36.

BAVARIAN MINT ICING

1 cup brown sugar, packed
3 Tbls. butter
3 Tbls. milk
½ cup chocolate chips
1 tsp. mint flavoring

Combine brown sugar, butter and milk in saucepan and heat to boiling, stirring. Remove from heat and stir in chips and flavoring.

DROP

DROP

Take a spoonful of soft dough, push it off onto a cookie sheet and bake it to a golden brown and you have a drop cookie, the type which fills more cookie jars than any other kind. The dough can be filled with many kinds of excellent surprises, the flavor and size can vary, but the shape is consistently round. Here are some excellent examples of the kind of homemade cookies people of all ages enjoy.

HAPPY FAMILY COOKIES

1 cup margarine
2 cups sugar
3 eggs
1 cup grated carrot
1 apple, ground
1 orange, ground
1 cup dates, ground
1 cup raisins, ground
4½ cups flour
1 tsp. soda
1½ tsp. cinnamon
¼ tsp. nutmeg
1 cup chopped nuts

Combine ingredients in order given. (Orange may be ground with peel on or off, as desired.) Drop by teaspoonsful onto greased cookie sheet. Bake at 350 degrees for 10 minutes. Remove to rack to cool. Yield: 7 dozen.

PIONEER PETS

½ cup shortening
1 cup brown sugar, packed
1 egg
1 tsp. vanilla flavoring
2 1-oz. sq. unsweetened chocolate
½ cup mashed potatoes
1½ cup flour
½ tsp. salt
½ tsp. soda
¾ cup buttermilk
½ cup nuts

Cream shortening and sugar. Beat in egg and flavoring. Melt chocolate and stir into batter; add potatoes and beat well. Sift dry ingredients together and add alternately with buttermilk. (Add more flour if needed.) Stir in nuts. Drop on greased cookie sheet and bake at 400 degrees for about 10 minutes. Let stand a minute on sheet before removing. Frost with cocoa frosting if desired.

Cocoa Frosting

5 Tbls. cocoa
2 cups powdered sugar
3 Tbls. butter
Half-and-half

Combine ingredients using enough half-and-half to make of spreading consistency. Spread on warm cookies. (The pioneer cooks undoubtedly used real cream in this recipe.)

WALDORF SALAD COOKIE

2 ¾ cups flour
½ tsp. soda
¼ tsp. salt
1 tsp. cinnamon
1½ cups brown sugar, packed
¾ cup real mayonnaise
2 large eggs
1 tsp. vanilla flavoring
1½ cups chopped apple
1 cup chopped walnuts
½ cup chopped celery

Combine flour, soda, salt and cinnamon in bowl. Cream brown sugar, mayonnaise, egg and flavoring at medium speed in electric mixer. When light and fluffy, blend flour into creamed mixture at low speed. When smooth, add rest of ingredients. Drop by tablespoonful on ungreased cookie sheet. Bake at 350 degrees 10 to 12 minutes. Remove to wire rack to cool. Store in tight container.

FUDGE YUMMERS

2 cups graham cracker crumbs
1 can sweetened condensed milk
½ cup coconut
½ cup raisins
¼ cup sunflower seeds
1 tsp. vanilla flavoring
¼ cup cocoa

Combine ingredients. Drop by teaspoonful on greased cookie sheet.

Bake at 350 degrees for 10 minutes. (Brought to the KMA Festival by an 8-year-old girl.)

ORANGE CREAM CHIPS

2 ¼ cups flour
½ tsp. salt
1 cup vegetable shortening
1 cup sugar
3-oz. pkg. cream cheese
2 eggs
2 tsp. orange juice
1 tsp. grated orange rind
6-oz. pkg. chocolate chips

Sift flour and salt onto wax paper. Beat shortening, sugar and softened cream cheese in bowl until creamy. Beat in eggs one at a time. Add juice and rind; blend in flour mixture, stir in chips. Drop dough by teaspoonful on greased cookie sheet. Bake at 350 degrees for 12 minutes, or until light brown around the edges. Cool on racks. Frost with following:

Orange Cream Icing

2 cups powdered sugar
3-oz. pkg. cream cheese,
    softened to room temperature
1 tsp. orange juice
1 tsp. grated orange rind

Combine ingredients until well blended. Spread on cookies.

FLORIDA ORANGE DROPS

¾ cup sugar
⅔ cup shortening
1 egg
½ cup fresh orange juice
2 Tbls. grated orange peel
2 cups sifted flour
½ tsp. soda
½ tsp. baking powder
¼ tsp. salt

Cream sugar and shortening. Beat in egg. Add orange juice and peel. Combine dry ingredients and blend in. Drop on greased cookie sheet and bake at 375 degrees for 8 to 10 minutes. Frost with orange-powdered sugar frosting.

SUNSHINE DROP COOKIES

1½ cups brown sugar, packed
1 cup butter
2 eggs
1 cup sour milk or buttermilk
1 tsp. soda
½ tsp. salt
3¾ cups flour
2 tsp. baking powder
¼ cup fresh orange juice
1 Tbls. grated orange rind
1 tsp. vanilla flavoring

Cream sugar and butter. Beat in eggs. Combine sour milk or buttermilk and soda and set aside. Combine dry ingredients and sift. Add to creamed mixture alternately with sour milk mixture. Stir in remaining ingredients and beat until smooth. Drop by teaspoonsful onto greased cookie sheet. Bake at 375 degrees for 10 minutes. Frost.

Sunshine Orange Icing

2 cups powdered sugar
1 Tbls. butter
3 Tbls. orange juice
1 tsp. grated orange rind

Cream butter with half the sugar. Blend in juice and rind. Add enough more sugar to spread.

MINCEMEAT DROPS

1 cup sugar
½ cup butter or margarine
2 eggs
1 cup prepared mincemeat
2½ cups flour
1 tsp. baking powder
1 tsp. soda

Mix in order given. Drop on greased cookie sheet. Bake at 375 degrees for 8 to 10 minutes.

APRICOT UNBEATABLES

2 cups sifted powdered sugar
½ cup flour
½ tsp. baking powder
½ cup egg whites (3 to 4), unbeaten
2 cups chopped nuts
½ cup chopped dried apricots

Sift powdered sugar, flour and baking powder together. Combine with egg whites and beat with mixer until smooth. Stir in nuts and apricots. Drop by teaspoonful onto greased baking sheet. Bake at 325 degrees 15 to 18 minutes. Cool on racks.

PEPPERMINT CRISPS

¼ cup shortening
½ cup sugar
1 egg
1 cup sifted flour
½ tsp. baking powder
¼ tsp. soda
¼ tsp. salt
¼ tsp. nutmeg
1 Tbls. milk
3 to 4 Tbls. crushed peppermint candy

Cream shortening and sugar. Beat in egg. Sift dry ingredients together and beat into creamed mixture with milk. Drop by teaspoon on cookie sheet. Press with glass dipped in flour to flatten. Sprinkle tops with crushed candy.

Bake at 350 degrees 8 to 10 minutes. Cool slightly before removing from pan. Yield: 2½ dozen.

GUMDROP JEWELS

2 cups flour
1 tsp. baking powder
1 tsp. soda
1 cup margarine
1 cup brown sugar, packed
2 eggs
1 tsp. vanilla flavoring
1½ cups honey-flavored puffed wheat cereal
1 cup diced gumdrops

Combine flour, baking powder and soda. Cream margarine and brown sugar, beat in eggs and flavoring. Blend in flour mixture. Fold in cereal and gumdrops. Drop by teaspoonful on greased cookie sheet. Bake at 350 degrees for 10 minutes. Yield: 4 dozen.

CARAMEL APPLE COOKIES

½ cup shortening
1⅓ cups brown sugar, packed
1 egg
2¼ cups flour
1 tsp. soda
½ tsp. salt
1 tsp. cinnamon
1 tsp. cloves
½ tsp. nutmeg
1 cup grated, peeled apples
1 cup raisins
½ cup apple juice
1 cup chopped walnuts

Cream shortening and sugar; beat in egg. Sift dry ingredients together and add to first mixture. When well blended, stir in remaining ingredients. Drop by level teaspoonsful about 3 inches apart on greased cookie sheet. Bake at 350 degrees for about 12 minutes or until light brown. When cool, frost as follows:

Caramel Icing

¼ cup butter
¼ cup brown sugar, packed
1½ cups sifted powdered sugar
1/8 tsp. salt
2½ Tbls. half-and-half

Cook butter and brown sugar over medium heat until sugar dissolves (about 3 minutes). Add remaining ingredients and beat until smooth. Frost cookies. Excellent for cakes as well.

ORANGE CARAWAY DROPS

3 cups flour
2 tsp. baking powder
½ tsp. salt
2 eggs
1½ cups brown sugar, packed
1 cup mayonnaise
1 Tbls. grated orange rind
1 Tbls. caraway seeds
¾ cups buttermilk
1 tsp. soda

Combine flour, baking powder and salt. Cream eggs, sugar, mayonnaise, rind and seeds until fluffy. Stir buttermilk and soda together. Add dry ingredients alternately with milk, beating well. Drop by teaspoonsful on greased cookie sheet. Bake at 350 degrees for 10 minutes. While still warm, frost with the following icing:

Orange Icing

3 cups powdered sugar
¼ cup margarine
1 tsp. grated orange rind
Orange juice
1 tsp. lemon juice (optional)

Combine ingredients, using enough juice to make of spreading consistency.

PRUNE SPICE COOKIES

1 cup dried prunes
Water
½ cup shortening
1 cup sugar
2 large eggs, beaten
2 cups sifted flour
2½ tsp. baking powder
½ tsp. salt
1 tsp. cinnamon
½ tsp. nutmeg
¾ cup liquid (half milk, half
   prune liquid)

Cover prunes with water and let stand several hours. Simmer gently until tender. Drain; reserve liquid. Chop prunes and measure ¾ cup. Cream shortening and sugar. Beat in eggs. Sift flour with dry ingredients. Blend into creamed mixture alternately with liquid. Fold in prunes. Drop on greased cookie sheet by teaspoonful. Bake at 350 degrees for 10 minutes or until done.

COOKED CARROT COOKIES

1 cup sugar
¾ cup shortening
1 egg
1 cup cooked, mashed carrots
2 cups flour
2 tsp. baking powder
¼ tsp. salt
1 tsp. vanilla flavoring

Beat ingredients together in order given. Drop by teaspoonful on greased cookie sheet. Bake at 375 degrees for 12 minutes or until done. Orange icing is very good on these cookies.

YELLOW CUCUMBER COOKIES

½ cup oil
½ cup white sugar
1 cup brown sugar
2 eggs
1 tsp. butter flavoring
1 tsp. vanilla flavoring
2 cups flour
2 tsp. baking powder
½ tsp. soda
1 tsp. cinnamon
2 cups rolled oats
1 cup raw yellow cucumber,
   peeled, seeded and ground
½ cup nuts

Cream oil and sugars; beat in eggs and flavorings. Stir in remaining ingredients and mix well. Drop on greased cookie sheet and bake for about 15 minutes at 350 degrees.

SWEET POTATO COOKIES

3 cups sugar
1½ cups shortening
3 tsp. vanilla flavoring
3 cups cooked and mashed sweet
    potatoes
½ cup sweet potato water
5 cups flour
3 tsp. soda
3 tsp. baking powder
3 tsp. cinnamon

Combine ingredients in order given, blending in flour alternately with potato water to make dough stiff enough to drop by teaspoonsful on ungreased cookie sheet. Bake at 325 for about 15 minutes. Yield: 6 dozen.

＜＝＝＝＝＝＞

ZUCCHINI CHOCOLATE FLATS

½ cup shortening
1⅓ cups brown sugar, packed
1 egg
3 cups flour
½ tsp. salt
1 tsp. soda
2 Tbls. cocoa
¼ cup milk
1 cup shredded zucchini
1 cup raisins

Cream shortening and sugar, beat in egg. Combine flour, salt, soda and cocoa; mix half into creamed mixture, then stir in milk, zucchini and raisins. Beat in rest of flour mixture. Drop by teaspoon on a greased cookie sheet. Bake at 350 degrees for 8 to 10 minutes. Frost with chocolate frosting if desired.

＜＝＝＝＝＝＞

APPLESAUCE DELIGHTS

2½ cups flour
½ tsp. salt
1 tsp. soda
½ tsp. instant coffee
¼ cup margarine
½ cup sugar
1 egg
1½ cups applesauce
¾ cup chopped walnuts
12-oz. pkg. butterscotch chips

Combine dry ingredients. Cream margarine and sugar, beat in egg. Blend in dry ingredients alternately with applesauce. Stir in nuts and chips. Drop on greased cookie sheet and bake at 350 degrees for 12 to 15 minutes. Sprinkle with powdered sugar while hot.

CHOCOLATE CHUNK COOKIES

½ cup butter or margarine
½ cup white sugar
¼ cup brown sugar, packed
1 tsp. vanilla flavoring
1 egg
1 cup flour
½ tsp. salt
½ tsp. soda
2 German sweet chocolate bars
1⅓ cup flaked coconut

Beat first five ingredients together until light and fluffy. Combine dry ingredients and stir in. Break chocolate into chunks (not too small) and add along with coconut. Chill 1 hour. Drop by heaping teaspoonsful onto greased cookie sheet. Bake at 350 degrees for 12 to 15 minutes until brown. Interesting change from chips.

BUTTERMILK CHOCOLATE CHIP DROPS

½ cup shortening
1 cup brown sugar, packed
1 tsp. vanilla flavoring
1 egg
1¾ cups flour
½ tsp. soda
½ tsp. salt
¼ cup buttermilk
6-oz. pkg. chocolate chips

Cream shortening and sugar together. Beat in flavoring and egg. Sift dry ingredients together and add alternately with buttermilk. Stir in chips. Drop by teaspoon on greased cookie sheet. Bake at 350 degrees for about 8 minutes.

CHOCOLATE FROSTIES

1 cup brown sugar, packed
½ cup butter
½ cup milk
1 egg
1 tsp. vanilla flavoring
2 1-oz. sq. unsweetened chocolate, melted
1½ cups flour
½ tsp. soda
½ cup nuts

Cream sugar and butter together. Beat in milk, egg and flavoring. When well mixed, stir in melted chocolate. Add flour and soda. Fold in nuts. Drop by teaspoon on greased cookie sheet. Bake at 375 degrees for about 8 to 10 minutes. Do not overbake. Cool and frost with the following:

Frosting

1-oz. sq. unsweetened chocolate, melted
1½ oz. cream cheese, softened
1 Tbls. milk
Powdered sugar

Combine chocolate and cream cheese. Blend in milk and enough powdered sugar to spread.

DOUBLE CHIP COOKIES

¾ cup butter or margarine
1 cup white sugar
½ cup brown sugar
1 tsp. vanilla flavoring
2 eggs
2 cups flour
1 tsp. soda
2 cups milk chocolate chips
1 cup peanut butter chips

Cream butter and sugars together. Add flavoring and eggs and beat until fluffy. Stir in flour and soda. Add chips. Drop by teaspoonful onto ungreased cookie sheet. Bake at 350 degrees for 10 minutes or until slightly brown. Let stand two minutes, then put on racks to cool. Yield: 5 dozen.

HONEY CHOCO-CHIP DROPS

1⅓ cups shortening
½ cup honey
1 egg, beaten
1¼ cups flour
½ tsp. salt
½ tsp. soda
½ cup chocolate chips
½ cup nuts

Mix ingredients in order given. Drop by teaspoon on greased cookie sheet. Bake at 350 degrees for about 8 minutes. Watch closely. Honey browns more quickly than sugar.

HONEY-PEANUT BUTTER GOODIES

1 cup shortening
1 cup honey
1 cup white or brown sugar, packed
2 eggs
1 cup peanut butter
2½ cups sifted flour
½ tsp. salt
1 tsp. soda

Cream shortening and honey. Beat in sugar. Add eggs and mix well. Stir in peanut butter. Combine dry ingredients and mix in until smooth. Use a rounded measure of mixture for each cookie. Place on greased cookie sheet. Press with fork. Bake at 350 degrees for 10 to 12 minutes.

CORNFLAKE MACAROONS

2 egg whites
¼ tsp. salt
1 cup sugar
¼ tsp. almond flavoring
1 cup coconut
2 cups cornflakes

Beat whites until frothy, add salt and beat until stiff. Add sugar gradually, beating, until stiff peaks form. Fold in remaining ingredients. Drop on greased baking sheet. Bake at 350 degrees 12 to 15 minutes. Remove at once.

HONEY-DATE DROPS

1 cup sugar
1 cup honey
2/3 cup shortening
3 eggs
1/2 tsp. butter flavoring
1 tsp. vanilla flavoring
3 3/4 cups flour
1 tsp. soda
1 tsp. salt
1 cup sour cream
1 to 2 cups diced dates

Cream sugar, honey, shortening, eggs and flavorings until light and fluffy. Sift dry ingredients together and add alternately with sour cream. Fold in dates. Drop on greased cookie sheet. Bake at 375 degrees for 10 to 12 minutes. Dough keeps well for four or five days in refrigerator.·

DATE FLAKE COOKIES

1 cup flour
1/2 tsp. baking powder
1/2 tsp. soda
1/4 tsp. salt
1/3 cup butter or margarine
1/2 cup white sugar
1/2 cup brown sugar, packed
1 egg
1 tsp. vanilla flavoring
1 cup oat flakes
1/2 cup chopped dates

Mix dry ingredients together. Cream butter and sugar. Beat in egg and flavoring. Stir in flour mixture, cereal and dates. Drop on greased cookie sheet and bake at 375 degrees for 8 to 10 minutes. (Other cereal may be used if desired.) Yield: 2 1/2 dozen.

CREAM CHEESE COOKIES

1 cup butter or margarine
2 3-oz. pkgs. cream cheese
1 cup sugar
1 tsp. vanilla flavoring
1/4 tsp. salt
1 egg
2 Tbls. milk
2 cups flour
3/4 cup chopped peanuts

Cream together butter and cream cheese (softened to room temperature), sugar, flavoring and salt. Beat in egg and milk. Add flour. Fold in peanuts. Drop from teaspoon onto ungreased cookie sheet. Bake at 350 degrees for 15 minutes or until done. Remove to wire rack to cool. (Note: No leavening is in this recipe.)

DATE PUFFS

2 egg whites
1 cup powdered sugar
1 cup chopped dates
½ cup chopped walnuts
1 cup flaked coconut

Beat whites until stiff and dry. Beat in powdered sugar gradually. Stir in rest of ingredients. Drop on greased cookie sheet. Bake at 250 degrees about 20 minutes.

SOUTHERN CREAM COOKIE

1 cup margarine
2 cups sugar
3 beaten eggs
1 tsp. vanilla flavoring
1 cup sour cream
5 cups flour
½ tsp. salt
3 tsp. baking powder
½ tsp. soda
1½ cups nuts

Cream shortening and sugar. Add beaten eggs, flavoring and sour cream. Mix well. Add dry ingredients which have been sifted together. Stir in nuts. Drop from teaspoon on greased cookie sheet. Press with fork dipped in water to keep from sticking. Bake at 350 degrees for about 15 minutes. Yield: 8 dozen.

BUTTERSCOTCH DROPS

½ cup shortening
1½ cups brown sugar
2 eggs
1 cup sour cream
1 tsp. vanilla flavoring
2¾ cups flour
½ tsp. soda
½ tsp. baking powder
½ tsp. salt

Combine ingredients in order given. (You can make your own sour cream: mix ½ cup evaporated milk with 2 Tbls. vinegar.) Chill dough, drop on greased cookie sheet. Bake at 350 degrees for 8 to 10 minutes. Frost with browned butter-powdered sugar frosting.

CHOCOLATE WALNUT PUFFS

2 egg whites
1/8 tsp. salt
½ cup sugar
½ tsp. vinegar
½ tsp. vanilla flavoring
1 cup chocolate chips, melted
¾ cup chopped nuts

Beat egg whites with salt until foamy. Gradually beat in sugar until stiff peaks form. Beat in vinegar and flavoring. Fold in melted and cooled chocolate and nuts. Drop on greased cookie sheet and bake at 350 degrees for 10 minutes.

PINEAPPLE TINY TIMMIES

1 small can crushed pineapple
½ cup butter or margarine
1 cup brown sugar, packed
1 egg
2 cups flour
2 tsp. baking powder
½ tsp. salt
6-oz. pkg. butterscotch chips
½ cup chopped walnuts

Drain pineapple well, reserve juice. Cream butter and sugar together. Beat in egg. Blend in dry ingredients. Stir in 3 tablespoons reserved pineapple juice. Fold in pineapple, chips and nuts. Drop on ungreased cookie sheet and bake at 350 degrees for 12 minutes. Remove immediately and cool on rack.

GLAZED PINEAPPLE COOKIES

15½-oz. can crushed pineapple
2 cups sifted flour
1½ tsp. baking powder
¼ tsp. soda
¼ tsp. salt
½ cup margarine
1 cup brown sugar, packed
1 egg
1 tsp. vanilla flavoring
¼ tsp. pineapple or orange flavoring
½ cup pecans

Drain pineapple well, reserve juice for glaze. Sift dry ingredients together.

Cream margarine and sugar; beat in egg and flavorings. Stir in pineapple alternately with flour mixture. Fold in nuts. Drop by teaspoon on greased cookie sheet. Bake at 400 degrees for about 8 minutes. Glaze with the following:

Pineapple Glaze

1¼ cups powdered sugar
Pineapple juice

Combine sugar with enough juice to make a thin glaze.

DUMPY PINEAPPLE DROPS

1 cup shortening
1 cup brown sugar, packed
1 cup white sugar
2 eggs
1 cup undrained crushed pineapple
1 tsp. vanilla flavoring
1 tsp. soda
4 cups flour
1 cup chopped nuts

Dump first 6 ingredients into bowl. Mix on high with mixer until fluffy and smooth. With mixer on low, dump in remaining ingredients and blend well. Drop on greased pan. Bake at 400 degrees about 8 minutes.

CHOCOLATE PIXIES

1 cup shortening
2¾ cup sugar
½ cup cocoa
4 eggs
2 tsp. vanilla flavoring
4 tsp. baking powder
½ tsp. salt
½ cup oat flour*
2¾ cups white flour

Cream first five ingredients well. Blend dry ingredients together; stir in. Drop on greased cookie sheet; bake at 350 degrees for 10 to 12 minutes. *To make oat flour, put rolled oats in blender or processor and blend until fine.

◆━━━━◆

SPICY APPLE-RAISIN DROPS

½ cup butter
1 cup brown sugar, packed
2 eggs
¼ cup milk
2 cups sifted flour
1 tsp. baking powder
½ tsp. salt
1 tsp. cinnamon
½ tsp. cloves
½ tsp. nutmeg
1½ cups peeled, chopped apple
1 cup raisins
½ cup chopped black walnuts

Cream butter, sugar and eggs. Blend in milk. Combine dry ingredients and mix in until smooth.

Fold in rest and drop by teaspoon on greased cookie sheet. Bake at 375 degrees for 10 to 12 minutes. Frost if desired.

◆━━━━◆

APPLE PEANUT BUTTER GOODIES

½ cup white sugar
½ cup brown sugar, packed
½ cup shortening
½ cup peanut butter
1 egg, beaten
½ cup peeled, grated apple
1½ cups flour
¼ tsp. soda
¼ tsp. baking powder

Cream sugars, shortening and peanut butter. Blend in egg. Stir apple into dry ingredients and fold into batter. Drop by teaspoon onto greased cookie sheet and bake at 350 degrees for 12 to 25 minutes.

◆━━━━◆

SIMPLE DROP COOKIES

1 cup butter or margarine
½ cup sugar
1 cup flour
1½ cup rolled oats

Cream butter and sugar. Blend in flour. Stir in enough rolled oats to make dough to drop by teaspoon on greased cookie sheet. Bake at 350 degrees about 12 minutes. Roll in powdered sugar.

BLACK WALNUT COOKIES

2 cups sugar
2 cups lard or margarine
1 cup sour milk
1½ cups molasses
1 tsp. soda
½ tsp. cinnamon
½ tsp. cloves
½ tsp. ginger
½ tsp. salt
1 cup black walnuts
Flour to make soft dough

Cream sugar and shortening. Stir in milk and molasses. Blend dry ingredients and stir in; add nuts. Stir in enough flour to make of dropping consistency. Drop on greased cookie sheet. Bake at 350 degrees about 12 minutes.

OLD-FASHIONED MACAROONS

3 egg whites
¾ cup sugar
1 cup coconut
½ tsp. vanilla flavoring
½ tsp. almond flavoring

Combine ingredients in saucepan and cook over low heat, stirring, until mixture is thick (ditch will hold when knife is pulled through mixture)--about 10 minutes. Drop by half teaspoons on greased cookie sheet. Let stand 12 minutes. Bake at 300 degrees for 20 minutes or until light brown. Store in tight container.

1850 SPICE COOKIES

1 cup brown sugar
1½ cups sorghum or molasses
1 cup lard or butter
1 large or 2 small eggs
2 tsp. soda
¼ tsp. salt
2 tsp. ginger
1 tsp. cinnamon
1 tsp. nutmeg
½ cup hot water
5 cups flour (stone ground if possible)

Cream shortening, sorghum and sugar. Add eggs. Add soda and spices to hot water. Mix into batter; add flour to make of drop consistency. Drop on ungreased pan and sprinkle with sugar. Can "splat flat" with glass dipped in sugar. Bake at 375 degrees for 8 to 10 minutes. Yield: 8 to 9 dozen.

MAN PLEASERS

1 cup plus 2 Tbls. shortening
1 cup plus 2 Tbls. sugar
1 cup light molasses
2 eggs, beaten
4 ¾ cups cake flour
1 Tbls. baking powder
½ tsp. salt
2 tsp. soda
2 cups coconut
2 cups chopped walnuts
1½ cups raisins
1 cup milk

Cream first four ingredients until light and fluffy. Combine dry ingredients with coconut, nuts and raisins. Add to creamed mixture alternately with milk. Drop by tablespoonful on greased cookie sheet. Bake at 375 degrees for about 10 minutes.

LEMON DROP COOKIES

2 cups sifted flour
3 tsp. baking powder
½ tsp. salt
1 cup crushed candy lemon drops
¼ cup shortening
½ cup raisins
1 egg, beaten
½ tsp. vanilla flavoring
⅓ cup milk

Sift dry ingredients together. Crush lemon drops fine in four portions and stir the crushed candy immediately into flour to keep from sticking. Cut shortening into flour-lemon drop mixture. Add raisins. Combine remaining ingredients and stir into flour mixture. Drop by teaspoonsful onto greased cookie sheet. Bake at 350 degrees about 15 minutes. Yield: 3 to 4 dozen.

Evelyn Birkby (on the right), with the assistance of Virginia Miller of Randolph, Iowa, arranges plates of cookies, entries in the Shaped Cookie division of KMA's Fall Festival Cookie Contest.

INDEX

BAR COOKIES

DROP COOKIES

FILLED COOKIES

FROSTINGS AND FILLINGS

Farewell

Evelyn Birkby has been a Midwest writer and radio homemaker for many years. She and her husband Robert live in Sidney, Iowa, and are the parents of three grown sons. Her interest in recipes came about from necessity. At first her cooking was primarily to put food on the table and to keep the cookie jar filled, then she began experimenting with food ideas to use with her column writing and broadcasting. The writing and editing of cookbooks for Radio Station KMA has been a natural outgrowth of this interest in foods and their preparation.

Evelyn Birkby is the author of:

KMA'S FESTIVAL COOKIE BOOK

COOKING WITH KMA:
Featuring 60 Years of Radio Homemakers

KMA'S COME AGAIN COOKIE BOOK

And also,

ADVENTURE AFTER SIXTY;
Alone Through England and Scotland

A-Z
OF
STUMPWORK

INSPIRATIONS BOOKS

a granatum

EDITOR
Sue Gardner

EDITORIAL TEAM
Marian Carpenter, Lizzie Kulinski

DESIGN AND LAYOUT
Lynton Grandison

ILLUSTRATIONS AND PATTERNS
Kathleen Barac

PHOTOGRAPHY
Andrew Dunbar

REPROGRAPHICS
PrintX Digital

PUBLISHER
Margie Bauer

DISTRIBUTION ENQUIRIES
Country Bumpkin Publications
315 Unley Road, Malvern
South Australia 5061 Australia
Phone: 08 8372 7600
Fax: 08 8372 7601
Email: marketing@countrybumpkin.com.au
Website: www.countrybumpkin.com.au

PRINTED AND BOUND IN CHINA

A - Z OF STUMPWORK
ISBN 0-9750920-5-7

Copyright ©2005 Country Bumpkin Publications
Reprinted June 2005